WONDER

An Advent and Christmas Collection

Andy March

Halwill Publishing

First published in Great Britain in 2022 by Halwill
Publishing,
99 Buckingham Rise, Coventry CV5 9HF

ISBN 978-1-7398051-1-1

A CIP catalogue record for this book is available from the
British Library.

Cover design: Andy March

Cover image: "Blue Nativity" by Adyna

Contents

Part 2 – Proclaiming Good News – sermons during Advent and Christmas

Part 3 – Responding to the Story

Part 4 – Reflecting on the Story

<u>Foreword</u>

The joy of writing, when you shake off the norms and the preconceived, is that really you can write whatever you want to.

'Unclassified' isn't a low grade - it's a sign of pioneering out-of-the-boxmanship.

Andy March has done that with this book. Having preached at his church, I've seen first-hand Andy's commitment to people and kingdom ideas, telling the old, old story in new and innovative ways.

This new work is the fruit of Andy's labours working 'in the trenches' of local church. It drips with experience, wit and wisdom - an impressive addition to his growing output and legacy.

For devotion and inspiration, via his own perspiration, here you'll find a one-stop shop for Christmas word feasting. An advent calendar of tasty word; a buffet of delectable sound bites. Don't get too fat, now, will you?

Andy Kind, Comedian and Author

Introduction

I love Christmas. I think I look forward to it almost as much as my children. I love almost everything about it – the cheesy music; the lights that illuminate the dark December streets; the carol services and nativity plays; the carols and Bible readings; going to church at really strange times of the night; the Christmas trees and decorations … I could go on.

I love telling stories – particularly Bible stories – and finding ways for these timeless and ancient truths to hit home today, whether for a hall full of schoolchildren, an all-age congregation, or occasional visitors to church at carol services. If I can find a different way to convey essential truths, I will, even if it involves looking silly (which it often has, as I've dressed up as angels, wise men and even adorned donkey ears, much to the embarrassment of my children!).

This book is the fusion of these two passions and the result of a decade or so of my work in Church of England parish ministry. Most of these pieces have been written for church all-age and carol services as well as "ordinary" Sundays, and school services. They were written to be read aloud and performed, so you may want to try this yourself!

Whether you're someone looking for fresh inspiration as you plan your own services, or a Christian looking for something to inspire your own worship and devotion, I hope this book is a blessing to you.

Wonder is not designed to be read front-to-back like a novel. See it more as a selection box to be dipped into and enjoyed.

Part 1 – Telling the story

A collection of monologues and sketches that seek to tell the familiar story in a new way, often from the perspective of the characters involved. These would be perfect for use in services and would work as stand-alone pieces.

Part 2 – Proclaiming Good News – the message of Advent and Christmas

Sermons I have preached over the years. The "Carols by Candlelight" sermons try to reflect the year's events in some way and link it to a particular aspect of the Good News of Christmas.

Part 3 – Responding to the Story

Poetry, which often forms my personal expression of worship in this season. My greatest challenge as a "professional Christian" is that I can be so focused on communicating the Good News to others that I fail to appreciate its meaning for myself. These poems flow from those times when I stop, reflect and worship.

Part 4 – Reflecting on the Story

An Advent and Christmas devotional that starts on 1st December and ends 6th January, containing Bible verses I selected and reflections I wrote on Twitter. You may want to use this to accompany your own devotions, perhaps at the end of the day.

Please get in touch and let me know what you've found helpful, particularly if you've used any of these pieces in your own context. Get in touch via email – info@halwillpublishing.co.uk – I'd love to hear from you.

As a vicar, I genuinely believe I have one of the best jobs in the world. I love having the opportunity to express my creativity to tell other people about Jesus. I'm grateful to my church community, St Christopher's Allesley Park and Whoberley in Coventry, for your love and support over the years and putting up with some of my more whacky ideas; to the wonderful school community of St John's Church of England Academy, especially the brilliant children and also to the headteachers whom I've had the privilege of serving with

– Andy Brown, Gary Watson and Laura Stevenson, who have been friends as well as colleagues. Thanks to Andy Kind for writing the foreword, and Simon Ponsonby who saw my vocation as a writer. Thanks to all the preachers and authors, such as Adrian Plass, Dan Schaeffer, Tim Keller, Ian Paul, who have inspired my thinking, writing and creating on Advent and Christmas. I have tried to cite direct references, but I apologise if I've missed any out. Thanks to my parents, who have been my editors-in-chief over the years; and to my mother-in-law, Janet Wilson, who has always been such an encouragement to me in my ministry. I want to especially thank my family – my wife, Liz, who gives me space and grace to do what I do and holds the family together while I'm busy with church things (Christmas time is not an easy time for vicarage families) and my children, who have been so supportive and among my biggest fans. I love you all.

Ultimately, my gratitude is to Jesus, the reason for the season, my hope and my song. "May I never lose the wonder of your mercy".

Andy March
Coventry
November 2022

PART 1
Telling
the
Story

Elizabeth and Zechariah

[5] In the time of Herod king of Judea there was a priest named Zechariah, who belonged to the priestly division of Abijah; his wife Elizabeth was also a descendant of Aaron. [6] Both of them were righteous in the sight of God, observing all the Lord's commands and decrees blamelessly. [7] But they were childless because Elizabeth was not able to conceive, and they were both very old.

[8] Once when Zechariah's division was on duty and he was serving as priest before God, [9] he was chosen by lot, according to the custom of the priesthood, to go into the temple of the Lord and burn incense. [10] And when the time for the burning of incense came, all the assembled worshippers were praying outside.

[11] Then an angel of the Lord appeared to him, standing at the right side of the altar of incense. [12] When Zechariah saw him, he was startled and was gripped with fear. [13] But the angel said to him: 'Do not be afraid, Zechariah; your prayer has been heard. Your wife Elizabeth will bear you a son, and you are to call him John. [14] He will be a joy and delight to you, and many will rejoice because of his birth, [15] for he will be great in the sight of the Lord. He is never to take wine or other fermented drink, and he will be filled with the Holy Spirit even before he is born. [16] He will bring back many of the people of Israel to the Lord their God. [17] And he will go on before the Lord, in the spirit and power of Elijah, to turn the hearts of the parents to their children and the disobedient to the wisdom of the righteous — to make ready a people prepared for the Lord.'

[18] Zechariah asked the angel, 'How can I be sure of this? I am an old man and my wife is well on in years.'

[19] The angel said to him, 'I am Gabriel. I stand in the presence of God, and I have been sent to speak to you and to tell you this good news. [20] And now you will be silent and not able to speak until the day this happens, because you did not believe my words, which will come true at their appointed time.'

[21] Meanwhile, the people were waiting for Zechariah and wondering why he stayed so long in the temple. [22] When he came out, he could not speak to them. They realised he had seen a vision in the temple, for he kept making signs to them but remained unable to speak.

[23] When his time of service was completed, he returned home. [24] After this his wife Elizabeth became pregnant and for five months remained in seclusion. [25] 'The Lord has done this for me,' she said. 'In these days he has shown his favour and taken away my disgrace among the people.'

(Luke 1:5-25)

"He's taken away my shame" – Elizabeth's Story

Well, hello everyone, my name is Elizabeth. I used to be known as "sad Elizabeth" because myself and Zechariah were unable to have any children, and *everyone* knew that it was my body that wasn't working, not Zechariah's.

What's that, Zechariah? You didn't tell them that? No, I know, you never made me feel bad, but I do feel guilty, because it's true, and you'd make a wonderful father …

Anyway, people used to look at me rather pityingly and the social invitations dried up, because all everyone in the village seemed to have to talk about was their family life, what their kids and then grandkids were up to, and we couldn't exactly share in these conversations so, to avoid the awkwardness of having to find a different topic of conversation, people simply stopped inviting us over. It's sad, really, because I do so love children, and wouldn't have minded being someone's honorary aunty or loving someone else's child, given the chance.

Oh no, it's not good to be childless in this community. You get strange looks, like you're some sort of outsider. People also think that you've been cursed by God – that being childless is some sort of punishment. Of course, we both prayed fervently for children, with tears, many times over many years, until we knew it was both too late. But I still love my Lord and I know he loves me. Both Zechariah and I have walked with God our whole lives and we've sought to follow him as faithfully as we could. We're both descended from Aaron, you know – Zechariah serves as a priest in the temple, he belongs to the priestly division of Abijah – and he's very proud about it, aren't you Zechariah.

Sorry, I should say that Zechariah is here with me, he just can't talk at the moment, which is why you're only hearing from me. Normally I wouldn't get a word in edgeways – sorry, that's a joke – actually, it hasn't made that much difference to conversation at home.

Ok, now Zechariah's rolling his eyes, and gesturing to me – I think he wants me to get on with it.

Ok, where was I? So, Zechariah is a priest. Each division takes turns to be on duty at the temple, to help in the day-to-day running of that wonderful place, a week at a time. There are lots of priests who serve in lots of different ways, and each role is decided by lot. Zechariah was thrilled when the lot was cast and he had the privilege of burning incense at the table of incense, which stood in the holy place, as close as any ordinary priest could get to the holy of holies. It was a once-in-a-lifetime experience for him.

So, he was burning the incense while people were praying outside, when something extraordinary happened.

An angel of the Lord appeared, standing at the right side of the altar. Dear Zechariah was terrified – I don't blame him! Angels aren't as cute and cuddly as they're made out to be, are they, dear?

What's that? He was that big?

The angel – he called himself Gabriel – tried to reassure him and told him not to be afraid. Then he said something unbelievable. "Your prayer has been heard. Your wife Elizabeth will bear you a son, and you are to call him John. You'll be overflowing with joy – but you won't be the only ones – many will delight in his birth. He's going to be great in God's eyes, filled to bursting with the Holy Spirit. Many will come back to God through him, there'll be reconciliation in families because of him; he'll get the people ready for God."

Zechariah was gobsmacked, weren't you, dear? He simply couldn't believe it, so he said to the angel, "Do you expect me to believe this? I'm an old man and my wife is an old woman."

– this wasn't the cleverest thing you ever said, was it dear, he was an angel, after all!

The Angel wasn't impressed with that at all – he replied, "I am Gabriel. I stand in the presence of God, and I have been sent to speak to you and to tell you this good news. But because you won't believe me, you'll be unable to say a word until the day your son is born. Every word I've spoken to you will come true in time – God's time."

While all this was happening, the people were waiting for Zechariah and wondering why he was taking so long, but when he finally came out, he couldn't speak, so he had to try and gesture to them using some sort of sign language, and they twigged that he must have seen a vision or something.

When he came home having finished his duty at the temple, apparently unable to say a word, clearly he had a lot of explaining to do – I wondered at first if it was some sort of trick he was playing because he was bored of talking to me – we have been married an awful long time, you know – but he sat and wrote down everything that had happened. Well, when I read it, I was speechless.

Oh, sorry, poor choice of words.

Ok, I was dumbstruck … that's not any better, is it?

How about gobsmacked? Not much of an improvement …

Ok, well, I simply couldn't believe it – and wouldn't believe it, if it weren't for the proof that is growing inside me.

We're going to be parents – I'm going to be a mum. They won't be calling me sad-Elizabeth anymore. God has been so kind to us. He's taken away the shame of having no children.

Zechariah can't wait either, although I may miss the peace and quiet when he's able to talk again!

Mary and Gabriel

²⁶ In the sixth month of Elizabeth's pregnancy, God sent the angel Gabriel to Nazareth, a town in Galilee, ²⁷ to a virgin pledged to be married to a man named Joseph, a descendant of David. The virgin's name was Mary. ²⁸ The angel went to her and said, 'Greetings, you who are highly favoured! The Lord is with you.'

²⁹ Mary was greatly troubled at his words and wondered what kind of greeting this might be. ³⁰ But the angel said to her, 'Do not be afraid, Mary, you have found favour with God. ³¹ You will conceive and give birth to a son, and you are to call him Jesus. ³² He will be great and will be called the Son of the Most High. The Lord God will give him the throne of his father David, ³³ and he will reign over Jacob's descendants for ever; his kingdom will never end.'

³⁴ 'How will this be,' Mary asked the angel, 'since I am a virgin?'

³⁵ The angel answered, 'The Holy Spirit will come on you, and the power of the Most High will overshadow you. So the holy one to be born will be called the Son of God. ³⁶ Even Elizabeth your relative is going to have a child in her old age, and she who was said to be unable to conceive is in her sixth month. ³⁷ For no word from God will ever fail.'

³⁸ 'I am the Lord's servant,' Mary answered. 'May your word to me be fulfilled.' Then the angel left her.

Mary visits Elizabeth

³⁹ At that time Mary got ready and hurried to a town in the hill country of Judea, ⁴⁰ where she entered Zechariah's home and greeted Elizabeth. ⁴¹ When Elizabeth heard Mary's greeting, the baby leaped in her womb, and Elizabeth was filled with the Holy Spirit. ⁴² In a loud voice she exclaimed: 'Blessed are you among women, and blessed is the child you will bear! ⁴³ But why am I so favoured, that the mother of my Lord should come to me? ⁴⁴ As soon as the sound of your greeting reached my ears, the baby in my womb leaped for joy. ⁴⁵ Blessed is she who has believed that the Lord would fulfil his promises to her!'

Mary's song

⁴⁶ And Mary said:

'My soul glorifies the Lord
⁴⁷ and my spirit rejoices in God my Saviour,

⁴⁸ for he has been mindful
of the humble state of his servant.
From now on all generations will call me blessed,
⁴⁹   for the Mighty One has done great things for me —
holy is his name.
⁵⁰ His mercy extends to those who fear him,
from generation to generation.
⁵¹ He has performed mighty deeds with his arm;
he has scattered those who are proud in their inmost thoughts.
⁵² He has brought down rulers from their thrones
but has lifted up the humble.
⁵³ He has filled the hungry with good things
but has sent the rich away empty.
⁵⁴ He has helped his servant Israel,
remembering to be merciful
⁵⁵ to Abraham and his descendants for ever,
just as he promised our ancestors.'
⁵⁶ Mary stayed with Elizabeth for about three months and then returned
home.
(Luke 1:26-56)

The following three passages take different
approaches to the same famous Bible story – the
annunciation (or the visit of the Angel Gabriel to the
Virgin Mary) – the first two were written as a "straight"
monologues and the third, inspired by the work of
Adrian Plass, is more satirical and definitely less
canonical!

"May His will be done" – Mary's Story

Do you ever wonder whether something's really happening to you, or if it's just a dream? Well, a few months ago, I was at home, doing my chores when I looked up and a man was standing there. He'd just appeared out of nowhere. Light shone from him; I was dazzled by him. I was terrified. And then he spoke to me,

"Greetings, favoured woman, the Lord is with you!"

I was troubled and confused. I had no idea what he meant or who he was. He spoke again,

"It's ok, Mary, don't be scared. You've got nothing to fear. I'm Gabriel, God's messenger. God sees your heart. He knows how much you love him. He has a surprise for you. You're going to become pregnant and give birth to a son. He's going to have the name, Jesus. He will be great, the Son of God – one day he'll be king forever.

I was stunned, but managed to blurt out, "H-how? How is this possible? I've never been with a man."

The angel replied, "The power of God will come upon you. The child inside you will be called Holy one, son of God. Nothing is impossible for God. Even your relative, Elizabeth has become pregnant in her old age! She's six months pregnant already, and she'll have a baby boy. You see, God's word will never fail."

You might wonder how I felt in that moment. Was I still scared? Absolutely. But that wasn't all. It may seem unbelievable to you but there was peace in my heart, as well as a feeling of joy that was bubbling up inside of me.

The angel seemed to be waiting for my response. What could I possibly say to him? I felt calm enough to answer, "I am the Lord's servant. May everything you have said about me come true."

And just like that, the angel left me.

Next morning, I wondered if this had all been a dream. After all, what the angel had said was simply unbelievable - impossible, even. How could it be true? But then I remembered the angel's words about Elizabeth. Pregnant? Wow, she was old enough to be a grandmother. Could she really become a mother at her age?

There was only one way to find out. I asked mum and dad for permission to travel to visit her and Zechariah - it had been a long time since we'd seen them, after all.

The long walk gave me plenty of time to think and pray. I love my Lord. I would do anything to serve him. I couldn't believe that this was the task he had for me – a mere girl, nobody important. And then, of course, there was Joseph. We're due to be married next year. The whole village is talking about it – everyone's been invited. But what will happen now? Will he still want to marry me once he discovers my news? I wouldn't blame him if he didn't. On my journey I poured out all these thoughts to God.

When I arrived, Elizabeth greeted me, and there she was – heavily pregnant. It was true! God had done the impossible, just as the angel had said! We embraced, and Elizabeth cried out,

"How God's blessed you and your child, Mary! Why am I so honoured to be visited by the mother of my Lord? When I saw you, my baby jumped for joy. You're blessed because you believed that God would do what he said!"

This time I couldn't contain myself, the joy burst out of me,

"My soul praises God, my Spirit rejoices in my Saviour! He's noticed me, a lowly servant girl, and done great things for me. I AM so blessed!"

It hadn't been a dream after all. This is really happening. I'm going to be the mother of the Saviour. God's done the impossible in me. I know he will give me the strength to do his will.

I don't know how dear Joseph will react, if he'll stay with me, or what my parents will say, but I trust that God will carry me through. May his will be done.

The Messenger

Hi everyone, can you tell what I am? That's right, I'm an angel – not just any angel – my name is Gabriel. You might have heard of me. Do you know what I do – apart from look magnificent, that is – do you like my wings?

Anyway, I work for the great I am, the beginning and the end, the creator, the Almighty One – but you'll probably know him simply as God. I'm one of God's messengers – whenever he has something important he wants to tell people, he asks me to pay them a visit. You see, God has a really big soft spot for humans, although I don't really know why. I mean, he shows them so much love and care, gives them an amazing world to live in, he shows them rules and guidelines to help them to live well, and they completely ignore him. They fight each other, even kill each other over such silly things. And yet he still reaches out to them, still loves them like your mum or dad loves you – even when they mess up and get things wrong.

It's amazing really. The thing is, God saw that they were getting into such a mess and we – that's the other angels and myself – we were saying to him, look, give up – they're not going to listen – they're not worth it. But he looked at us with love, and said, "I can't give up. People are too special. I made them to love like me … I can't bear to watch them hurt each other and hate each other. I need to show them that there is another way – a way of love and forgiveness – and I think there is only one way I can do this. I need to show them in person. I need to become one of them." We all gasped … it was such an incredible thing to do – it was so risky – but we had no idea just how risky, just how crazy it was. We thought that if he was going to become a human, he would come as a king – after all, he is the king of all kings. But we were very wrong!

"Gabriel," God said, "I want you to pay a special visit. I want you to visit someone who's going to be my earthly mother. I want you to visit a girl called Mary, in Nazareth." I was surprised, because all the important people lived in Jerusalem, in the palace, "But, my Lord, isn't he going to be a king?" I asked. "Yes," he replied, "but not the kind of king you think he's going to be. If I come as a king, if I'm born in a palace, it'll just show that only the so-called important people matter.

And then, when I've been born, I want you to go to the shepherds outside Bethlehem. I need to be like one of them. They always get forgotten. They always get rejected. They need to know that I've not rejected them. In fact, I've come for them. I need every person – even the very poorest person – to know that they matter to me. That every person is precious to me. Maybe they'll be more likely to listen to me and learn to love each other. Maybe there'll be hope for the world."

I was amazed – in awe, really. "You really do love them, don't you? But it's so risky! What if they don't listen? What if they still hate each other? What if they still hate you?" Something in his look told me he'd already thought about this. He really must be crazy about these humans. If only they knew how much God loves them!

Anyway, I'd better get going... got some rather special news to share with a certain young girl called Mary.

An Unexpected Visitor

Has it ever occurred to you how incredible Mary was? I'm not sure that many people would have been willing to be part of what, if you really think about it, was a crazy idea. She can teach us a great deal about costly obedience and radical faith. I wonder if Mary was the first young woman Gabriel had visited. But just imagine if Mary had not been the first young woman Gabriel had visited ... I wonder what might have happened?

God sent the angel Gabriel to Nazareth, a town in Galilee, to a young woman, whose name was Mildred. The angel went to her and said, "Greetings, you who are highly favoured! The Lord is with you."

Mildred was greatly troubled at his words and wondered what kind of greeting this might be. But the angel said to her, "Do not be afraid, Mildred; you have found favour with God. You will conceive and give birth to a son, and you are to call him –"

"You what?" Mildred exclaimed, "Favour with God? Having a baby? you're having a laugh – I'm just a girl – that's impossible!"

"Well," Gabriel replied, getting a bit cross, "I was going to get onto that before you interrupted, so, if I may go on ... You are to call the baby Jesus. He will be great and will be called the Son of the Most – "

Mildred interrupted once more, "Yeah, yeah, yeah – so, he's going to be important – you've still not answered my question ... how's this going to happen – can we just skip to that bit, please?"

Gabriel sighed. "If you had let me finish, I was about to tell you ..."

"Well, go on," Mildred said, arms crossed, "I'm all ears ... this better be good," she muttered under her breath.

"I heard that!" Gabriel retorted, "Anyway, as I was about to say, it's going to be God's baby – "

"Can I just stop you there –" Mildred interjected.

"If you must," Gabriel replied warily.

"Honestly, you're off your rocker!" Mildred exclaimed, "It's a loopy idea. I've never heard anything so crazy in all my life – in fact, it's the stupidest plan I've ever heard."

"So, you're not going to do it?" Gabriel asked with disbelief, "Even though you're highly favoured?"

"That's right, "you've found the wrong young woman – Now get out of my house!" Mildred shouted, opened the door and ushered the bemused angel out of her house.

Gabriel sighed. He pulled a pen and crumpled piece of paper out of his pocket. The paper had a list of names on it. "Another one bites the dust," he muttered, "God won't be pleased. Can't say I'm too surprised though, it does seem like a bit of a crazy plan to me, but what do I know, I'm just the messenger! Who's next? There can't be many more virgins in Nazareth!" Gabriel looked down at his paper once more, "Oh, Mary. I hope we have better luck with her."

Of course, that is not what happened! I've just been having a bit of fun which I hope illustrates how special Mary was in accepting her calling – I believe that Mary was the only one chosen to have the daunting, but incredible privilege of carrying the Son of God, and that when God chose her, he knew that she would accept the role as Jesus' mother. I believe she was only able to, because God gave her the strength. I believe that God will give us the strength to do the things he asks of us. Let's pray for that strength now.

Joseph and the Donkey

¹ In those days Caesar Augustus issued a decree that a census should be taken of the entire Roman world. ² (This was the first census that took place while Quirinius was governor of Syria.) ³ And everyone went to their own town to register.

⁴ So Joseph also went up from the town of Nazareth in Galilee to Judea, to Bethlehem the town of David, because he belonged to the house and line of David. ⁵ He went there to register with Mary, who was pledged to be married to him and was expecting a child. ⁶ While they were there, the time came for the baby to be born, ⁷ and she gave birth to her firstborn, a son. She wrapped him in cloths and placed him in a manger, because there was no guest room available for them.

(Luke 2:1-7)

¹⁸ This is how the birth of Jesus the Messiah came about[d]: his mother Mary was pledged to be married to Joseph, but before they came together, she was found to be pregnant through the Holy Spirit. ¹⁹ Because Joseph her husband was faithful to the law, and yet[e] did not want to expose her to public disgrace, he had in mind to divorce her quietly. ²⁰ But after he had considered this, an angel of the Lord appeared to him in a dream and said, 'Joseph son of David, do not be afraid to take Mary home as your wife, because what is conceived in her is from the Holy Spirit. ²¹ She will give birth to a son, and you are to give him the name Jesus,[f] because he will save his people from their sins.'

²² All this took place to fulfil what the Lord had said through the prophet: ²³ 'The virgin will conceive and give birth to a son, and they will call him Immanuel'[g] (which means 'God with us').

²⁴ When Joseph woke up, he did what the angel of the Lord had commanded him and took Mary home as his wife. ²⁵ But he did not consummate their marriage until she gave birth to a son. And he gave him the name Jesus.

(Matthew 1:18-25)

A Donkey's Tale

Hello, my name's Darrell, the donkey. You'll never guess what happened to me the other day... I was in Nazareth minding my business eating grass, thinking very important donkey thoughts, and that sort of thing, when Joseph came up to me, looking rather flustered. He told me we were going on an adventure to Bethlehem.

Now, donkeys may be a bit slow, but I know that Bethlehem is a long way from Nazareth. I began to realise that would be hard work. And then Joseph told me that we wouldn't be going alone ... that Mary would be coming with us. I don't mean to be rude, but Mary was ... how do you put it ... very pregnant ... she was heavy – and Joseph wasn't going to carry her all that way, was he? No, that would be my job. And what reward would I get? A few carrots, that's all.

So, I wasn't very pleased, but I like Joseph and I know that he loves Mary very much. He's been a good master for me, and I could see that he really needed my help, so I agreed to go.

It was a long and dusty road to Bethlehem. Mary wasn't that heavy, I suppose. Joseph tried to hide it, but I could tell he was worried about her; the baby could come at any moment. Then I heard them say something that made my ears prick up. I heard Mary say that she hoped God's baby wouldn't be born in the desert, and that a palace would be far more suitable. I stopped in my tracks and looked at them – God's baby? What could they mean?

And then they told me the whole story – the visit from the angel, the strange but wonderful news that Mary had been chosen by God to be the mother of the new-born King and saviour of the world and that God had asked Joseph to look after her. Well, I felt a bit guilty for being so grumpy about carrying Mary. I now knew I was so honoured to bear such a special burden.

When we got to Bethlehem, we found there was no room for us to stay. I couldn't believe it. I felt like shouting out and telling them just whom I was carrying! But then I remembered that I can't talk. Mary and Joseph just prayed and held hands tightly. Finally, we found a stable to stay in. It wasn't ideal – I mean, I didn't mind staying there – I am a donkey, after all – but it's no place for a normal person, let alone a king.

And that's where the baby was born. They called him Jesus. I could tell he was special just by looking at him. Mary didn't have much time to rest, because we had some unexpected visitors – some shepherds – rough looking blokes they were, and a bit smelly too. We were alarmed at first, but then we heard their incredible story. They'd been told that angels had appeared as they were watching their flocks and told them he had wonderful news – a baby had been born in Bethlehem, that he was a very special baby born for all the people. They were amazed that the angel had chosen to tell them, of all people, because no one thinks they're important, but God must think that they are.

It's been an amazing few days. Days I'll never forget. Something really special has happened. This baby's been born to tell us that ordinary people – and ordinary donkeys – matter to God. If he's God, he could have chosen to be born anywhere at any time. But he chose to be born in a stable – and I got to carry him all the way to Bethlehem. Now that really is amazing!

Joseph's Story

Hi everyone, my name's Joseph and I've been asked to tell you the story of the most incredible thing that's ever happened to me. I'm an ordinary carpenter from Nazareth, in Galilee, the north of the country. I was excited – I'd just got engaged to Mary, a beautiful girl from the village, so my head was full of plans and preparation – I was beginning to build the home we'd live in when we got married, and I made sure there was enough room for us, and God-willing, our children. And things were going so well. That was until Mary came over one day and told me she had some news. She was going to have a baby. And I wasn't the dad. I couldn't believe it. I thought it was a joke. She told me that an angel visited her and told her she'd be having God's baby, that it was a miracle. She swore she was telling the truth, but I didn't … couldn't believe her. I was so angry. I needed to be alone. I needed some time to think. I couldn't believe it. I had so much hope for our future. It was all gone now. I couldn't marry her now, not after what she has done. But I loved her. I didn't want her to suffer more than necessary. I decided to break off the engagement quietly. People didn't need to know.

But then I had a dream. An angel appeared to me. Said he was called Gabriel, that he was a messenger sent from God. He told me not to break off the engagement. Don't hesitate to get married. That Mary was telling me the truth. God's holy spirit made her pregnant. She was carrying God's special baby – a boy. When he was born, we were to call him Jesus, which means God saves – because he would come to save his people from the all the mess and hurt they get themselves into. That baby boy would be known as Immanuel – which means God is with us. That baby boy would need an earthly dad to look after him, and Mary would need a good, faithful husband. God had a special job for me to do. I didn't know what to say. I couldn't believe it. But I did. The angel told me not to be afraid. God can give you the strength you need. So, I made it up with Mary, and we got married.

Months passed, and the day of our son's birth drew near. All was going to plan, until we received some unwanted mail. The emperor ordered that a census be taken of the whole empire. Everyone had to return to their ancestral hometown to be counted. My family's hometown is Bethlehem, which meant we had to make the four-day journey there ... not ideal for poor Mary, who was heavily pregnant.

So, when we got to Bethlehem, we were all exhausted, especially Mary. We didn't know if we'd be able to find somewhere to stay. I thought we would be ok somehow, because of the baby Mary was carrying. That baby was going to be the saviour, the King. God would look after us. I knew he was with us. We went to visit relatives, but they were full to bursting – lots of family members had come to stay because of the census, so they told us the guest room was full. But we could stay with them in the family quarter, although, it would involve being with the animals too. We didn't care where we stayed as long as it was clean, dry and warm. We were so relieved. God really was with us in that moment. And that's where Jesus was born. We wrapped him in cloths and laid him in a manger. It may seem like a funny place for Jesus to be born – it wasn't very private or special – he's a King, after all, but somehow it seemed right – he was born among the people – with ordinary people. He hasn't just come for so-called important people, but he's come for ordinary people – to save everybody and nobodies. The prince of heaven was born as an ordinary person. And I have the incredible privilege and responsibility of looking after him, of being his dad. It's daunting, but I know deep down it'll be ok, because God's with us and will help us, as he's done every step of this crazy journey so far.

Joseph and the Donkey (a sketch)

Joseph: Hi everyone, my name's Joseph and I've been asked to tell you the story of the most incredible thing that's ever happened to me. I'm an ordinary carpenter from Nazareth, in –

Donkey: [off stage] Ahem (coughing loudly).

Joseph: What was that? Anyway, I'm an ordinary carpenter

Donkey: Ahem - Hee-haw

Joseph: What's that? [Looks back]

Donkey: [Pop up] It's me. I didn't want you to forget about me. Everyone always forgets about me. They don't even say that there is a donkey in this story …

Joseph: I wasn't going to forget about you … anyway, you don't come into the story yet … Sorry everyone, where was I? Oh yes, I'm an ordinary carpenter

Donkey: And I'm his ordinary donkey …

Joseph: Yes, he's my ordinary donkey … Anyway, I'm

Donkey: Ahem!

Joseph: Ok, *we're* from Nazareth in Galilee, the north of the country. I was excited – I'd just got engaged to Mary, a beautiful girl from the village, so my head was full of plans and preparation – I was beginning to build the home we'd live in when we got married, and I made sure there was enough room for us, and God-willing, our children.

Donkey: Hee-haw

Joseph: What?

Donkey: You've forgotten someone

Joseph: Who?

Donkey: Me. You mentioned you and Mary, your children who hadn't even been born yet, but you didn't mention me ... told you, you always forget about your poor donkey.

Joseph: Ok, sorry. I was building the home we'd live in as a family, and include space for the donkey ...

Donkey: That's better!

Joseph: And things were going so well. That was until Mary came over one day and told me she had some news. She was going to have a baby. And I wasn't the dad. I couldn't believe it. I thought it was a joke.

Donkey: But it wasn't?

Joseph: Nope. She told me that an angel visited her and told her she'd be having God's baby, that it was a miracle. She swore she was telling the truth, but I didn't ... couldn't believe her.

Donkey: How did you feel?

Joseph: I was so angry.

Donkey: I know, I heard you shouting. You also threw some tools around, kicked a tree or two....

Joseph: Alright, alright, you don't need to tell the whole world... I was angry, yes. Also I needed to be alone. I needed some time to think. I couldn't believe it. I had so much hope for our future. It was all gone now. I couldn't marry her now, not after what she has done. But I loved her. I didn't want her to suffer more than necessary. I decided to break off the engagement quietly. People didn't need to know.

Donkey: But you didn't do that ...

Joseph: No.

Donkey: Why? What happened?

Joseph: I had a dream.

Donkey: A dream? Really? All my dreams are about carrots and grass, that sort of thing ...

Joseph: Well, my dream was a bit different. An angel appeared to me. Said he was called Gabriel, that he was a messenger sent from God. He told me not to break off the engagement. Don't hesitate to get married. That Mary was telling me the truth. God's holy spirit made her pregnant. She was carrying God's special baby – a boy. When he was born, we were to call him Jesus, which means God saves – because he would come to save his people from the all the mess and hurt they get themselves into. That baby boy would be known as Immanuel – which means God is with us. That baby boy would need an earthly dad to look after him, and Mary would need a good, faithful husband. God had a special job for me to do.

[Pause]

Joseph: Donkey. Is there something wrong?

Donkey: Why?

Joseph: You've not said anything.

Donkey: Well, I'm speechless.

Joseph: That's what I mean … that never happens.

Donkey: That was some dream!

Joseph: You're telling me! I didn't know what to say. I couldn't believe it. But I did. The angel told me not to be afraid. God can give you the strength you need. So, I made it up with Mary, and we got married.

Donkey: What happened then?

Joseph: Nothing for a while. Months passed, and the day of our son's birth drew near. All was going to plan, until we received some unwanted mail. The emperor ordered that a census be taken of the whole empire. Everyone had to return to their ancestral hometown to be counted.

Donkey: Wow, that's crazy … in fact, it's non-census! Gettit? He-haw Hee-haw

Joseph: Vey funny! Anyway, my family's hometown is Bethlehem, which meant we had to make the four-day journey there … not ideal for poor Mary, who was heavily pregnant…

Donkey: Or for me …

Joseph: Why?

Donkey: Because I had to carry her! It was very tiring, but I didn't mind, because I was carrying someone very special.

Joseph: And you didn't moan very much either! So, when we got to Bethlehem, we were all exhausted, especially Mary

Donkey: And me

Joseph: And you … and the baby was due soon, but we didn't know if we'd be able to find somewhere to stay. I thought we would be ok somehow, because of the baby Mary was carrying.
That baby was going to be the saviour, the King. God would look after us. I knew he was with us. We went to visit relatives, but they were full to bursting – lots of family members had come to stay because of the census, so they told us the guest room was full. But we could stay with them

in the family quarter, although, it would involve being with the animals too.

Donkey: And what's wrong with that?

Joseph: Nothing at all … we didn't care where we stayed as long as it was clean, dry and warm. We were so relieved. God really was with us in that moment. And that's where Jesus was born. We wrapped him in cloths and laid him in a manger.

Donkey: It's a funny place for Jesus to be born, isn't it?

Joseph: Why?

Donkey: It's not very private or very special. He's a king after all, isn't he?

Joseph: Actually, I think that it's a good place for Jesus to be born. He'll be born among the people – with ordinary people. He hasn't just come for so-called important people, but he's come for ordinary people – to save everybody and nobodies.

Donkey: And every donkey.

Joseph: Exactly! The prince of heaven was born as an ordinary person. And I had the incredible privilege and responsibility of looking after him, of being his dad.

Donkey: You know what

Joseph: No, what?

Donkey: I think you'll make a rather good job of it. God's with you and will help you, after all.

Joseph: Really, you think so?

Donkey: Yes, I do.

Joseph: Wow, donkey, I think that's the nicest thing you've ever said to me!

The Shepherds and the Angels

[8] And there were shepherds living out in the fields near by, keeping watch over their flocks at night. [9] An angel of the Lord appeared to them, and the glory of the Lord shone around them, and they were terrified. [10] But the angel said to them, 'Do not be afraid. I bring you good news that will cause great joy for all the people. [11] Today in the town of David a Saviour has been born to you; he is the Messiah, the Lord. [12] This will be a sign to you: you will find a baby wrapped in cloths and lying in a manger.'

[13] Suddenly a great company of the heavenly host appeared with the angel, praising God and saying,

[14] 'Glory to God in the highest heaven, and on earth peace to those on whom his favour rests.'

[15] When the angels had left them and gone into heaven, the shepherds said to one another, 'Let's go to Bethlehem and see this thing that has happened, which the Lord has told us about.'

[16] So they hurried off and found Mary and Joseph, and the baby, who was lying in the manger. [17] When they had seen him, they spread the word concerning what had been told them about this child, [18] and all who heard it were amazed at what the shepherds said to them. [19] But Mary treasured up all these things and pondered them in her heart. [20] The shepherds returned, glorifying and praising God for all the things they had heard and seen, which were just as they had been told.

(Luke 2:8-20)

What's so special about shepherds?
(A sketch)

SCENE 1

[THREE SHEPHERDS ASLEEP IN THE FIELDS, SNORING LOUDLY.]

[Enter GABRIEL, dressed in white suit.]

GABRIEL: Ahem! [coughs politely]

[SHEPHERDS still snoring loudly.]

[GABRIEL coughs louder. SHEPHERDS still asleep.]

GABRIEL: OI!

[SHEPHERDS grunt and stir, but sleep on.]

GABRIEL: There's only one thing for it. A bit of glory's called for. [CLAPS HANDS TWICE.]

[STAGE LIGHTS TURNED ON FULL.]

[SHEPHERDS wake up with a start, look wildly around, shocked, and scream.]

SHEPHERDS: AAH!

SHEPHERD 1:   Wh – wh – what's going on?

GABRIEL: Ahem!

[SHEPHERDS turn and face GABRIEL.]

SHEPHERDS: AAH!

GABRIEL: It's ok. Don't be afraid!

SHEPHERD 1: Don't be afraid? You'd be afraid if you were in our position. We were just minding our own business, watching our flocks by night –

GABRIEL: You were asleep actually –

SHEPHERD 1: - we were resting our eyes, weren't we boys?
[OTHER SHEPHERDS NOD]

SHEPHERD 1: umm, well, anyway ... we're looking after our sheep and then you appear out of nowhere, scaring us out of our wits with this bright light shining all around –

GABRIEL: It's the glory of the Lord, actually. Cool, isn't it?

SHEPHERD 2: Glory of the ... Wh – wh – who are you?

SHEPHERD 3: And where did you come from?

SHEPHERD 1: And could you turn the lights down a bit? We're being blinded here!

GABRIEL: Yes, yes, ok. [CLICKS FINGERS and LIGHTS dim.] That better? Good. I'm Gabriel, I come from heaven. I'm an angel.

SHEPHERD 2: Gabriel? An angel? From heaven?

GABRIEL: Yes, that's right – do you have to repeat everything I say? Anyway, I've been sent here by the Lord Almighty, creator of the universe, the Alpha and Omega, God himself to bring you a message.

SHEPHERD 2: Bring us a message? – oh, sorry, repeating you again, aren't I?

GABRIEL: That's quite all right. Where was I? Oh yes, I've come to bring you a message. Now where did I put it? [REACHES INTO POCKET] Here it is. CLEARS THROAT AND READS OUT.]

"I bring you good news that will cause great joy for all the people. Today in the town of David a Saviour has been born to you; he is the Messiah, the Lord. This will be a sign to you: You will find a baby wrapped in cloths and lying in a manger."

[FOLDS UP PAPER AND PUTS IT BACK IN POCKET. Looks at SHEPHERDS who stand with mouths wide open, staring blankly.]

GABRIEL: Hello? Did you hear what I just said?

SHEPHERD 1:   A Saviour has been born today, he's the Messiah, the Lord, there's great joy for all people – and you're telling us?

GABRIEL: Yes, is that a problem?

SHEPHERD 2:   Have you seen the state of us? Have you smelt us?

GABRIEL: Yes, what's wrong?

SHEPHERD 3:   [aside] He's not that bright for an angel, is he? [to GABRIEL] You see, the thing is, we're shepherds. We look after sheep in the fields. We smell like sheep. We're not very important. Are you sure you're in the right place? Did your heavenly sat-nav system go a little wrong?

GABRIEL: [aside] He's not very bright for a shepherd, is he? [to SHEPHERDS] No, I've not gone wrong. I meant to come all this way to see you, strange as it seems. I've come to give *you* the good news.

SHEPHERD 2:   Us?

GABRIEL: Yes, that's right. You. This baby that's been born is a very special baby. He's a king. Well, the King of Kings, and he's been born to save the world. He's been born for *everybody*, including smelly shepherds like your good selves. God Almighty himself wanted *you* to be the first to know. He happens to have a soft spot for shepherds.

[SHEPHERDS look at each other in amazement.]

SHEPHERD 1:   Can it be true?

SHEPHERD 2:   That a king has been born for us?

SHEPHERD 3:   Us nobodies?

GABRIEL: That's the point, actually. You're not nobodies. Not in God's eyes. In fact, nobody's a nobody. Everybody's special to God. That's why this baby's been born.

SHEPHERD 1:   Wow, that's amazing!

GABRIEL: Do you want to see him?

SHEPHERD 2:   Can we? But we're not dressed suitably!

GABRIEL: It's ok. Don't worry, go just as you are.

SHEPHERD 3:   And we don't have any gifts… What will his parents say?

GABRIEL: I really don't think they'll mind. I think they'll be pleased to see you. Go. It's ok. It really is good news for you.

SHEPHERD 2: Well, what are we waiting for? Let's go to Bethlehem and see this baby!

[SHEPHERDS run out as MUSIC PLAYS "Gloria in excelsis deo."]

SCENE 2

[STABLE at front of church with MARY and JOSEPH and ANIMALS around the manger.]

[SHEPHERDS run from back of church.]

SHEPHERD 3: are we nearly there yet?

SHEPHERD 1: Yes, yes, nearly.

SHEPHERD 2: In fact [POINTS TO FRONT OF CHURCH] There it is!

SHEPHERD 3: Wow, a real-life King. And we're going to meet him.

SHEPHERD 2: Quiet now, he could be asleep.

[SHEPHERDS walk towards STABLE on tiptoes. MARY and JOSEPH sitting down, Jesus in manger.]

SHEPHERD 1: Hi, you might think we're crazy, but an angel told us to come here. He said that a king's been born today and that we'd find him here. Is that him? Can we have a look?

[SHEPHERDS gather around MANGER.]

SHEPHERD 2: Wow, that's amazing. He's amazing.

SHEPHERD 1: It's really true.

SHEPHERD 3:   God's in that manger.

[SHEPHERDS bow down in worship.]

SCENE 3

SHEPHERDS run to back of church, saying excitedly "Have you heard? It's amazing! A king's been born – for you and me!" etc.

"We all matter to God" – The Shepherd's Story

It's the most incredible news! You'll never believe what I've seen tonight. It's just incredible, I can't believe it!

Well, me and the other guys, we were out in the fields outside Bethlehem, watching our flocks by night – no, watching our flocks, not washing our socks – anyway, we were minding our business, watching our flocks, counting sheep, that sort of thing, when suddenly this figure all dressed in white appeared. We were just minding our own business, watching our flocks by night – we've been told by the shepherd's union to say that we were definitely *not* sleeping, but were, in fact, resting our eyes. Anyway, this figure in white appeared out of nowhere, the whole hillside was lit up brightly and we were scared stiff! This figure told us not to be afraid, which is a bit of a joke, cos he'd be scared if he were in our shoes, anyway, he said that he was an angel called Gabriel, and he'd come from heaven, sent by God especially to give us a message. The message was amazing. He said he'd come to bring a message of good news that will cause great joy for all people. He said a saviour had been born to us – the Messiah – the Lord. He then said that we'd find this saviour wrapped in cloths and lying in a manger – that this is how we'd know what he's said about him is true.

I couldn't believe it! I either thought I'd gone mad, or that someone had put something in my cocoa, or that he'd got lost and ended up in the shepherd's fields by mistake. I was most definitely gobsmacked! I mean, why was an angel visiting us at all, let alone visiting us to give us this message? I mean, we're just shepherds. We look after sheep in the fields. We smell like sheep. We're not very important. I can't even get my mother-in-law to visit me, let alone an angel. Surely there had been a mistake? But no, the angel assured us there was no mistake. He meant to come all this way to see us, to come and give us the good news. Apparently, this new baby is a very special baby. A king – the king of kings, born to save the save the world. He's been born for *everybody*, including smelly shepherds like me, ordinary people like you and me. God wanted us to be the first to know.

I couldn't believe it. It's incredible – a king has been born for us. Us nobodies. But I guess that's the point. I think that's what the angel was trying to tell us. Nobody's a nobody in God's eyes. Everybody's special to God. That's why this baby's been born.

We were just taking it in when suddenly this whole choir appeared and began singing the most beautiful song I've ever heard, singing about Glory to God and peace on earth. It was wonderful, and I didn't want it to end. Then when they finished their song, Gabriel said we could go and visit the baby. I couldn't believe that either – I mean, we weren't dressed in a way fit for a king. Amazingly, we could come as we were. We didn't have any presents for him or the new parents. But Gabriel didn't think that mattered either.

And so, we smelly shepherds visited the new-born king tonight. I even held him in my arms. God was in that manger. God was in my arms. It's just so amazing. It really is good news for me. It's good news for you too. We're all special to God. We matter to him. That baby has been born for you and for me. It's just amazing! Anyway, I've got to go – got some other people to tell!

Simeon

[25] *Now there was a man in Jerusalem called Simeon, who was righteous and devout. He was waiting for the consolation of Israel, and the Holy Spirit was on him.* [26] *It had been revealed to him by the Holy Spirit that he would not die before he had seen the Lord's Messiah.* [27] *Moved by the Spirit, he went into the temple courts. When the parents brought in the child Jesus to do for him what the custom of the Law required,* [28] *Simeon took him in his arms and praised God, saying:*

[29] *'Sovereign Lord, as you have promised,*
you may now dismiss your servant in peace.
[30] *For my eyes have seen your salvation,*
[31] *which you have prepared in the sight of all nations:*
[32] *a light for revelation to the Gentiles,*
and the glory of your people Israel.'

[33] *The child's father and mother marvelled at what was said about him.* [34] *Then Simeon blessed them and said to Mary, his mother: 'This child is destined to cause the falling and rising of many in Israel, and to be a sign that will be spoken against,* [35] *so that the thoughts of many hearts will be revealed. And a sword will pierce your own soul too.'*

(Luke 2:25-35)

"A Promise-keeping God" – The Song of Simeon

I have always loved the Scriptures, ever since I was a boy. When I was young, I was drawn to the heroism of people like Moses and David, and even Gideon, who rose to lead their nations to victory against their enemies. I knew their stories off by heart. I prayed every night that a new David would rise up to take down to the Goliath of the Roman empire. I resented their iron rule, enforced by those soldiers everywhere.

My parents often spoke of their hope that God would send a rescuer, a liberator to free us. They showed me passages in the prophets that spoke of this figure who would come – someone anointed by God himself – and establish God's rule and reign. When I was a teenager, I scoffed at them. "It's been 400 years since these promises were spoken – longer even. How sure are you that God hasn't forgotten us?" Yet, their faith never wavered. I was irritated by their stubbornness to hold onto what clearly seemed like a fantasy, but another voice within me seemed to whisper, "look for yourself. How sure are you that this is fantasy?" This voice wouldn't go away, so I read the Scriptures myself, particularly the prophets. I kept on reading them. Words about a child being born, who would be called Wonderful Counsellor, Mighty God, Everlasting Father, Prince of Peace, whose reign of justice and righteousness would never end. Also, a suffering servant who would bear the punishment for all the sin and injustice that is so evident all around us, the sacrificial lamb whose wounds would bring healing and freedom. The more I read these promises, the more convinced I became that they would come true – and then, one day I heard that voice again – quiet, yes, but insistent. "You will see this promise being fulfilled." Was it my imagination? I began to think so as the weeks, months and then years passed by. There were moments of excitement when I was in the temple courts at times of prayer. I would look around, wondering if the man or boy I was looking for was present and then have that familiar wave of disappointment as I realised that the wait would go on just a little longer. After a while when I went to the temple, I no longer had that same sense of excitement. I wondered, was I mistaken, after all? Had it just been wishful thinking, nothing more? But deep down, that light never went out. I couldn't let go of hope completely. I knew somehow that God hadn't forgotten his promises to his people – he remembered and rescued us when we were slaves in Egypt, and when we were in exile, we were brought back home. God would come to the rescue again. I knew it. And I somehow knew, for whatever reason, that I would see the Rescuer, the Messiah, myself.

Then, it happened. This morning, soon after I woke up that voice within me spoke once more. Just one word. "Today." I was astonished. Really? How will I know? "You'll know," that voice replied. "Go." So, I went. What was I looking for? I still didn't really know, but I trusted that the same voice would guide me. I rushed to get ready then ran to the temple. Once I was there, I looked around fervently until – I saw them. A young couple, with a baby in their arms. There was nothing special about them whatsoever. They looked like an ordinary couple, but there was nothing ordinary about them or the baby they were carrying. I knew immediately – this was the one. I could have wept with joy. I went up to them. "Excuse me," I said, "I know I'm a complete stranger, but I've been waiting for this day for many years. Your child is no ordinary baby." They quickly recovered from their initial shock at being addressed in this way and then told me their story that began with the angel's visit in Nazareth to his birth in Bethlehem just over a month beforehand. "His name is Jesus," the man finished, "the angels told the shepherds that he would be the Saviour, the promised

Messiah." I smiled and told them, "I know that to be true. A voice inside, who I now know to be the Spirit of God told me that I would see the Lord's Messiah. And you're holding him in your arms. May I hold him myself?" I asked.

"Of course," the mother replied, and handed over this helpless scrap of humanity. This helpless child was the one who would bring hope to Israel. I was bursting with joy and wonder and let out a song of praise.

"Now, Lord, you can let me, your servant, die in peace as you said.

I have seen your Salvation with my own eyes. You prepared him before all people. He is a light for the non-Jewish people to see. He will bring honour to your people, the Israelites."

I could tell Jesus's parents were amazed at what I was saying about him. As I handed him back, I spoke a prayer of blessing over them both, then looked at the mother and told her, "Many in Israel will fall and many will rise because of this child. He has been sent as a sign from God, but many will oppose him. As a result, the deepest thoughts of many hearts will be revealed. And a sword will pierce your very soul."

I could see the pain in her eyes when I said this, but also a sense of understanding too. She knew that not everyone would want to receive God's Messiah or welcome the message he would bring. "I know his path won't be easy," she replied, "But God will be with him and give him strength."

"As he will with you too," I answered, "You won't be alone. The light will never go out."

And with that I left them to get on with their day. I'd seen all I needed to see that day. God is a promise-keeping God. I have seen God's Salvation – held him in my arms. The Lord has come and delivered his people. Praise the Lord!

The Magi

2 After Jesus was born in Bethlehem in Judea, during the time of King Herod, Magi from the east came to Jerusalem ² and asked, 'Where is the one who has been born king of the Jews? We saw his star when it rose and have come to worship him.'
³ When King Herod heard this he was disturbed, and all Jerusalem with him. ⁴ When he had called together all the people's chief priests and teachers of the law, he asked them where the Messiah was to be born. ⁵ 'In Bethlehem in Judea,' they replied, 'for this is what the prophet has written:
⁶ "'But you, Bethlehem, in the land of Judah,
are by no means least among the rulers of Judah;
for out of you will come a ruler
who will shepherd my people Israel.'"
⁷ Then Herod called the Magi secretly and found out from them the exact time the star had appeared. ⁸ He sent them to Bethlehem and said, 'Go and search carefully for the child. As soon as you find him, report to me, so that I too may go and worship him.'
⁹ After they had heard the king, they went on their way, and the star they had seen when it rose went ahead of them until it stopped over the place where the child was. ¹⁰ When they saw the star, they were overjoyed. ¹¹ On coming to the house, they saw the child with his mother Mary, and they bowed down and worshipped him. Then they opened their treasures and presented him with gifts of gold, frankincense and myrrh. ¹² And having been warned in a dream not to go back to Herod, they returned to their country by another route.

(Matthew 2:1-12)

The Journey of the Magi

I hate camels. Hate 'em. If I ever see – or smell – another camel in my life, it'll be too soon. Grumpy, stubborn creatures. There's no moving them if they've really got the hump. My wife would say that they take after their masters, but I have no idea what she's talking about! Anyway, I've just got back from a long journey. I went with my colleagues, fellow astronomers – star-gazers – all the way to a small village called Bethlehem in Palestine, around a thousand miles away, far in the west. All because we saw a star. When you spend your life looking at the heavens like we do, you notice when something out of the ordinary appears. And this was just that. The brightest star we'd ever seen. We knew it was important. It just had to have appeared for some reason – stars like that don't appear for no reason. We consulted our scrolls and made an incredibly exciting discovery – this star meant that a new King had been born. Not just any King, but the Great King – the divine King of heaven.

Once we'd made that discovery, there was nothing for it – we had to go, to find out for ourselves if this was true. If it was, it changes everything. We made preparations, packed our bags, hired our camels and headed on the long journey. My wife says it was just an excuse to get away on a jolly for 6 months, but it wasn't. I would never have forgiven myself if I hadn't gone to Bethlehem to see this King. We wanted to meet him, to worship him.

There's not much to say about the journey. It was boring and uncomfortable, and sand got everywhere. The days were incredibly hot and the nights were ice-cold. But the whole journey, the star remained an ever-present guide for us, leading us on. Eventually we reached Jerusalem, which is where we figured a new-born King would be found. But he wasn't there. Instead, there was a grumpy old King – he would have got on with my camel – with a big chip on his shoulder, and he didn't seem at all pleased about the news of the birth of this baby King. I think we made a mistake in going to Jerusalem, because the star hadn't guided us there – we'd allowed our logic to overrule, and we'd gone slightly off course. Anyway, some advisers looked in their Scriptures and told us to go to Bethlehem, which is where the ruler would come. Herod, the grumpy old King seemed very concerned that we do our best to find this baby – he wanted to visit and pay his respects apparently, but I'm not sure we believed him. Anyway, we headed off and sure enough, our old friend the star reappeared when we set off from Jerusalem and we followed it the short distance to Bethlehem. We were so thrilled to see it again and to be able to follow it once more.

We arrived at the house where the baby and his parents were, and it was simply incredible – the parents, Mary and Joseph were very unsure about us at first but seemed reassured when we told them why we'd come. Apparently, we weren't the only unusual visitors they'd had. There'd been some shepherds who'd come from the hills outside Bethlehem, who'd been heralded by angels apparently. I wouldn't normally believe it, but there's nothing normal about what's happening. And when we arrived, there was this child, vulnerable but beautiful, ordinary, but there was no doubt something extraordinary about him. You could just sense it. Being in his presence took our breath away. We bowed down and worshipped him – it just seemed like the right thing to do. I can't describe how I felt in that moment – so full of joy, no longer tired, peaceful, and I felt the most overwhelming sense of love coming from him and love for him. In that instant I forgot the hundreds of miles we'd travelled and the incredible discomfort we'd felt – it was worth it to be there, in the presence of the King.

We gave him and his mother gifts – gold, to represent his kingship, frankincense, as a symbol of his future role as a priest who would speak to God on behalf of humanity – and myrrh, to symbolise that his death would be significant somehow. Mary and Joseph, his parents looked slightly baffled that ordinary peasants like them should be given such gifts, but that's the point – there was nothing ordinary about them.

We could have stayed there with this wonderful little family forever, but had to get back home. We had a dream warning us to keep clear of Herod on our way back, so we did. It was a long journey, but we didn't mind. It had been worth it, to be in the presence of the King of Kings himself. I've found what I've been searching for all my life and nothing can take that away from me. As for the camel, well, my wife tells me that I should become friends with him again – after all, I wouldn't have made the journey without him. I guess I'd better go and apologise for getting the hump with him.

Remembering with Mary

But Mary treasured up all these things and pondered them in her heart.
(Luke 2:19)

This series of reflections was written for a service that took place on the Sunday after Christmas. See Appendix One for a suggested service outline.

How it all began

I was an ordinary peasant girl in an ordinary village. I loved my family and I loved God. Life was good to me. I didn't have much, but never needed much. And I had a secure future – my family had found a husband for me – Joseph the carpenter, who was a good man – he loved God too, and I knew he would do his best to provide for me. I would hope to be a good wife to him, and a good mother to his children. That was the plan, anyway!

But everything changed when the angel came to visit. He said that God had chosen me for something wonderful. And then came the bombshell – he told me I was going to have a baby boy. His name would be Jesus. He'd be a king. I couldn't believe what I was hearing ... how would this be possible? I didn't know much about this sort of thing, but I was pretty sure that a man had to be involved somewhere. I'd never been with a man. To say I was surprised and shocked was an understatement! But then the angel told me that God would make it happen – that he would make the impossible possible – that God's holy spirit would be with me. I was amazed. I couldn't believe it, but I knew what he was saying was true. I was overjoyed and humbled. I wanted to be part of God's plan.

But then I had to tell Joseph and the rest of the family – I knew it wouldn't go down well. I mean – who would believe my story – would you? When I told him, he got up without a word, and left. He looked so hurt. I could tell he felt betrayed. That was the end of my marriage, then. It was no surprise when he came back and told me it was over. To be honest, I was just relieved to hear he wasn't going to make a big thing of it, that he wanted to divorce me quietly. It could have been so much worse – had the whole village found out, I would have been in a lot of trouble. My parents looked at me like they no longer knew me. Disappointed wasn't the word. I felt so alone. I hoped and prayed God would get me through this – he had, after all, got me into it!

*   *   *

Arriving in Bethlehem

He burst in, so excited, I had to tell him to slow down so I could understand what he was saying. He said that he'd had a dream. An angel had spoken to him, telling him that I had been telling the truth – that I would be having a son, that his name was Jesus and that he would save people from their sins. He told me he was sorry he doubted me and that he'd look after me and the baby, and be the best husband and father possible. I was so relieved. Everything would be ok after all.

The time came near for Jesus to be born. And then came another bombshell – we had to make a long journey to Bethlehem – a distance of 80 miles – to register for a census. I couldn't believe it. I began to panic, but Joseph reassured me. "It's ok," he said, "I'll make sure you're ok, and don't forget – God is with us."

And so, we began the long journey south to Bethlehem. It was hot and tiring and uncomfortable. I wondered if we'd make it on time. Would we get there before the baby was born? But I had to take comfort that every step we took we were a step closer to our destination. And finally, Bethlehem came into sight. We'd made it. But when we got there, we couldn't believe it – there was no room anywhere for us to stay. We were getting desperate, asking every guesthouse whether they had any rooms spare, but none did. Eventually, someone took pity on us and welcomed us in to stay with the animals. We were too relieved and grateful for that simple act of hospitality to care that it wasn't luxurious, but it was comfortable enough; and we'd be warm and dry, at least. God was looking after us, once again keeping to his promises.

*   *   *

The Visitors

We hadn't been parents for long when we suddenly had some visitors – some shepherds – you could tell by the smell! At first, we were quite intimidated – they looked quite rough, really. Not sure I wanted them around my baby. Joseph certainly looked like he didn't want to let them in. But then they told us their story – it was extraordinary... they were on the hillside outside of Bethlehem, tending their flocks when an angel visited them and told them all about Jesus – told them that he'd been born for ordinary people just like them. And then the sky was filled with a whole host of angels who sang praises to God – songs about peace on earth, songs of hope. They were told they'd find Jesus lying in a manger. So, they had to come, to find out if what the angel had told them was true – they'd wondered if they'd been imagining it; after all, shepherds so often get forgotten and overlooked. And they were overwhelmed when they found us; found him – the baby king who had been born for them. They spent time standing silently, just looking at this tiny baby – in awe at what they had been told and what all this meant. Then they left, praising God and telling everyone they met about what they had heard and seen that evening.

Later we had some even more mysterious visitors – magi from the east, who told us that they had travelled a thousand miles to visit my baby boy. They'd seen a special star, a star that told them a new king had been born. They travelled all this way to worship him. All the way to worship my child?? They'd brought some gifts with them – gifts of gold, frankincense and myrrh. Gifts to honour him. Gifts fit for a king. There really is something special about this boy. About my boy. I can barely believe all this has happened to me!

*   *   *

Mary's baby, God's son

If it weren't for the fact I cradled him in my arms, felt the joy and the pain of his birth, seen him grow up, I'd think this was all a dream – it'd be too wondrous, too unbelievable, really. Who could imagine that God would make himself known in such a way? Who could imagine that God would become human, become a tiny baby? Who could imagine that he'd love us so much that he'd become one of us? Who could imagine that this baby would be my own, that I would have been chosen to be the one to carry him inside me for those 9 months, to be chosen to care for him? I feel so honoured, so privileged, so humbled. God's own son is my son. It's unbelievable, and yet, it's true. God is with us. God loves us. Because of this baby, there is hope for the world. For you and me.

God's great Gift to All (a rhyming Nativity Play)

This was written during the Coronavirus Lockdown in 2020 when we were unable to meet together and do our usual Christmassy things, like nativity plays and services. Inspired by the phenomenon of video collaborations for worship songs like the blessing, I wrote a rhyming nativity play, which was performed to camera by over 20 members of our church. It was the perfect way for them to still feel involved during Christmas.

Scene 1

Narrator:
I want to tell you the story
Of how God left heaven's glory
He came to earth, became a man –
It's all part of his rescue plan

He came to save a world in pain
He came to bring us hope again
To show people both near and far
Just how completely loved we are

Want to know more? Then Come with me
To Nazareth in Galilee
Mary, though she doesn't know it
Will receive a special visit

Here comes the Angel Gabriel
God's messenger – why, can't you tell.

He's all in white with great big wings
Poor Mary jumps out of her skin!

Gabriel:
Mary, favoured one, God's with you!
Do not be scared, I have some news!
You're gonna have a baby boy
who'll save the world and bring great joy!

You'll call him Jesus – saving one,
He'll be King of Kings, God's own Son.

Narrator:
Mary gasped,

Mary:
Are you sure it's me?
I'm just a girl, how can this be?

Gabriel:
It'll happen through the Holy Spirit
For God's power knows no limit.

Narrator:
Mary replied,

Mary:
Oh wow, ok!
I am God's servant, I'll obey.

Narrator:
Off Gabriel went, job well done -
he'd found the mother for God's son.

Mary, meanwhile, she had to go
off to see her fiancé, Joe.

What would he say, what would he do
When she told him her shocking news?

Mary:
Something's happened, Joseph sweetie
that will change our lives utterly
I'm having a child, God's own son -
his precious gift for everyone,

Joseph:
I don't believe it, how's this true?
Mary, how can I trust in you?
What you've said is impossible
There's no future for us at all.

Narrator:
So, Joseph left, very upset
But fear not, it's not over yet.
An angel came to him that night
To help him get the story right.

Angel 1:
Joseph, Mary's story is true
And more than ever she needs you.
So, take her home to be your wife
To love and cherish all your life.

The baby that she's carrying
Means hope for all who are suff'ring
Give this child the name Jesus
He's Immanuel, God with us.

It means you'll never be alone
You'll never face life on your own.
For God's love will forever be
By your side for eternity.

Narrator:
Joseph nodded

Joseph:
God's will be done
I'll bring this boy up as my son.
With God's strength I will play my part.
I'll love this boy with all my heart.

Narrator:
With that the angel went away
while Joseph vowed that he would stay
no matter what by Mary's side
and they soon became groom and bride.

And here we'll leave the happy pair
for a moment so we can share
in a favourite Christmas song
and we'll be back before too long.

Scene 2

Narrator:
Nine months on Emperor Augustus
Decides to take a big census
across the empire every man
must go to the town of his clan
He does it to raise some money
Joseph doesn't find this funny

Joseph:
for we have to go far away
To Bethlehem, around four days
On foot or on a donkey's back
by Roman road or narrow track

Mary:
And all the while the day draws near
Until our baby will appear.

Narrator:
Will mum and baby be ok?
And will they find somewhere to stay?
A place fit for this baby king
Whose birth will such happiness bring?
Let's go now and go with them
to the little town of Bethlehem

Joseph
The town was busy, inns were full
There seemed to be no room at all
But we searched 'til we were able
To find lodgings in a stable.

Mary:
There he was born and wrapped in cloth
And placed in an animal trough.

Joseph:
Not ideal, but at least it's warm
We'll make sure he comes to no harm.

Narrator:
Mary and Joe looked on with love
At Jesus, the gift from above.

This child whose birth meant hope would dawn
For all in darkness, a new morn.

Stay with us now to find out who
Were first to hear of this great news.
Before that we will sing again
of peace on earth, goodwill to men.

Scene 3

Narrator:
Shepherds watching their flocks by night
Were soon to get an awful fright
Out of the darkness shone a light
Caused by an angel dazzling bright

The shepherds cried out,

Shepherds 1:
Whoa, what's that?

Narrator:
Terrified, they threw themselves flat.
The angel said,

Angel 2:
Don't be afraid
I bring good news for you today
news of great joy for all people
In Bethlehem a King's been born
A Saviour who is Christ the Lord
In whom all hope can be restored
This baby has been born for you.

This is how you will know it's true -
Go to Bethlehem where you'll find
This child who in a manger lies
wrapped in cloths and humility
He's there for you - go and you'll see!

Narrator:
A choir of angels filled the sky
Singing

Angels:
Glory be to God on high.

Peace on earth goodwill to all men

Narrator:
The shepherds get up there and then

Shepherd 1:
Let's go to Bethlehem right now
And see what we've been told about
Can what they've said be really true –
A king' been born for me and you?

Narrator:
They leave their flock and off they go
To see Jesus, Mary and Joe

Shepherd:
It's all as the angel has said -
Our King lies there in the straw bed.
We're filled with such wonder and joy
God's love lives in this baby boy.

Narrator:

Shepherds return shouting with glee
spread news of this nativity.
Meanwhile wise men come from afar

Wise men:
All this way we followed the star
that heralds the birth of a King
We've come to worship, gifts to bring

Gold, frankincense and precious myrrh -
Gifts fit for this, our rescuer.

Narrator:
Jesus' first guests may seem quite odd
But everyone matters to God
Whether you're rich or very poor
Whether you're near or very far
Whether you're big or very small.
Jesus is God's great gift for all.

this story's end is just the start
for this child can live in your heart.
Accept this gift at Christmas time
he'll stay with you for all your life.

So may you know wonder and joy
The great love of this baby boy.
And may you know deep in your heart
just how completely loved you are.

Immanuel: God with us (a Christmas Play)

This was written after reading an article by New Testament scholar Ian Paul that challenged the assumption we have that Jesus was born in a stable, "alone and isolated, with his family ostracised by the community."[1] He notes that there is no mention of a stable anywhere and it is more likely that the family guest room was full, because other relatives were staying there, and that Mary and Joseph would have stayed with Joseph's family, where Mary gave birth.

"The most natural place to lay the baby is in the hay-filled depressions at the lower end of the house where the animals are fed. ... In the Christmas story, Jesus is not sad and lonely, some distance away in the stable, needing our sympathy. Rather, he is in the midst of the family, and all the visiting relations, right in the thick of it and demanding our attention."

It got me thinking, what would a Christmas play look like if it took this seriously? How could you convey the wonderful truth that Jesus came to be God with us, in the midst of our loss, hurt and suffering? This is my attempt to answer this.

---

[1] Ian Paul, "Your seasonal reminder: Jesus was not born in a stable!", Psephizo: Scholarship. Serving. Ministry.
https://www.psephizo.com/biblical-studies/your-seasonal-reminder-jesus-was-not-born-in-a-stable/

Scene 1: St John's school

Narrator: Daniel was an ordinary boy with an ordinary life – mum, dad, baby brother, Sammy, and their dog, Barney. He was happy, he had fun at school, he had no worries, and no reason to worry. Then one day, everything changed. He was at school, on his way to lunch, when his headteacher came over to him.

Headteacher: Daniel [looking worried]

Daniel: Yes, Mr Watson, is everything ok?

Head: Actually, I need you to come into my office with me, if that's ok.

Daniel: Yes, of course. [they start to walk together]. Mr Watson?

Head: Yes, Daniel?

Daniel: Am I in trouble?

Head: No, no, it's nothing like that. You've done nothing wrong.

Narrator: Daniel had been a little worried before, but he was really worried now. What was the matter? A feeling of dread began to in the pit of his stomach. It grew when he saw that there was someone sitting in Mr Watson's office.

Head: Daniel, this is PC Bell.

Bell: Please, call me Sarah. Daniel, would you like to sit down?

Daniel: [sits down silently]

Bell: Daniel, there is no way of saying this gently, but I have some terrible news for you. Your mum and dad were in a car accident this morning.

Daniel: What about Sammy?

Bell: Sammy was there too.

Daniel: And Barney?

Bell: Barney?

Daniel: My dog ... was he there?

Bell: No, Daniel, he was at home. Daniel, your mum and dad are very sick. They were taken straight to hospital. The doctors are looking after them, and doing what they can, but we don't know if they're going to make it.

Daniel: And Sammy? What about Sammy?

Bell: Sammy's fine. He's a bit battered and bruised, but he'll be fine.

Head: [Puts his arm around Daniel] Daniel, I know this must be a terrible shock to you, but we'll do all we can to help. We've phoned your gran and granddad, and they're on their way to look after you. Your mum and dad are in good hands – they've got the best care possible.

Bell: I'm so very sorry, Daniel. I wish there was something I could do to make it better.

Narrator: Daniel sat there silently. Five minutes ago, his biggest worry was whether he'd have the time to eat his lunch and play football during the break. Now there was a chance that he may not see his mum and dad again. Life had changed forever. Nothing would be the same again. The rest of the day passed in a blur. Daniel went with Mr Watson and PC Bell to the hospital. He saw his mum and dad but didn't recognise them. He hated the beeps, and all the wires. Nice people in white coats came and spoke to him, and Gran and Granddad came to be with him and look after him and Sammy, but he couldn't listen to anything anyone was saying. There were only three questions he had, none of which anyone could answer. The first question was, were they going to get better? Would he be able to talk to them, to hug them again? The second question was, why? Why them? Why him? It was so unfair? The third question was about God. If he was there, why did he let that happen? Didn't he care? He felt so angry, confused, and alone.

That night, he was in bed, tossing and turning. Eventually, he fell asleep. The next thing he knew, he felt someone pulling at his pyjama sleeve. It was a boy around his age, all dressed in white.

Gabriel: Daniel – Daniel!

Daniel: [Murmuring] What is it?

Gabriel: Daniel!

Daniel: [still asleep, lying down] Yes? What? It's the middle of the night!

Gabriel: Wake up, Daniel – I have something important to tell you!

Daniel: What? [Looks up and sees the angel and sits up with a start] Who are you? How did you get in?

Gabriel: It's ok, Daniel, don't be afraid. My name is Gabriel. God's sent me to you.

Daniel: [wide awake now] God's what?

Gabriel: God's sent me to you. He's seen the pain you're in. He knows about your mum and dad. He knows you're angry with him, that you want to know if he cares.

Daniel: How does he know that? I haven't told anyone!

Gabriel: God loves you. He knows all about you. He knows all your thoughts. Anyway, he sent me to tell you that he does care, that you're not on your own. I know it's difficult to believe that at the moment. I'd like you to come with me. I've got something to show you. ...

[EXIT Gabriel and Daniel.]

Scene 2 – Heaven

Narrator: The next thing Daniel knew, he was in a room with figures all dressed in white, sat around at a table. One figure was wearing a crown. They were obviously in the middle of a discussion.

Angel 1: But there has to be something we can do – they're just killing each other. They're hurting each other. So many innocent people are suffering. And they completely ignore The King – pretend like he doesn't exist. They act like they're all kings, they don't love him or each other. It's just rude! We have to do something!

Angel 2: Why don't we write a message in the sky for everyone to read?

Angel 3: That's no good. They can just ignore it. I know, let's send legions of the angel army to teach them a lesson. They don't deserve the love that the King shows to them. If you ask me, I think you should give up on them. They're not going to listen to anything The King says.

The Prince: I won't give up on them. I can't give up on them. People are too special. I made them to love like me … I can't bear to watch them hurt each other and hate each other. I can't bear to watch the innocent suffer. I need to show them that there is another way – a way of love and forgiveness. I need to show them that I care, that I really am with them even as they suffer. And I think there is only one way I can do this. I need to show them in person.

Angel: And send a messenger? We've tried that before – look what happened to the prophets! No one listened to them. Why would they listen now?

The Prince: No. Not a messenger. I need to become one of them.

[ANGELS shake their heads in disbelief.]

Angel 2: But that's crazy!

Angel 3: Well, it might work if you come as an emperor or a king or something – show them who's boss.

Angel 1: Well, it's not right for the Prince of Heaven to be born in a palace.

Prince: I won't be born in a palace.

Angel 1: Well, that's a relief.

Prince: I'm going to be born among the animals, I'll be laid in a manger.

Angel: What??????

Angel 2: That's crazy!

Angel 3: Aren't you going to be born as a King?

Prince: Yes, but not the kind of king you think I'm going to be. If I come as a king, if I'm born in a palace, it'll just show that only the so-called important people matter. Actually, everyone matters to me.

[Prince looks to the side where he sees GABRIEL standing there.] Ah, Gabriel, I'm glad you're here. I have an important job for you.

Gabriel: Anything, my Prince.

Prince: I want you to pay a special visit. I want you to visit someone who's going to be my earthly mother. I want you to visit a girl called Mary, in Nazareth.

Angel 1: Are you sure about this? It's so risky.

Prince: People are worth the risk. Each and every one of them is precious to me. When they hurt, I hurt, when they weep, I weep. They're made in my image. I need to help them. I need to save them, and this is the only way I can. And Daniel.

Daniel: Who, me?

Prince: Yes, dear Daniel. Why don't you go with Gabriel. I'm sure he'd like some company.

Gabriel: Ok, then Daniel – come along ... we'd better get going.

Scene 3 – Nazareth – Mary's House

Narrator: And so, Gabriel went off to Nazareth to pay his special visit to Mary. Mary was a young girl in love. She'd just become engaged to her childhood sweetheart, Joseph. She was in the middle of daydreaming about their life ahead when she heard a voice calling. She was in for the surprise of her life.

Gabriel: Greetings Mary! God is so pleased with you, and he is with you!

Mary: [looking scared] Umm, I don't know what you mean. Who are you?

Gabriel: It's ok, Mary, don't be scared. You've got nothing to fear. I'm Gabriel, God's messenger. God sees your heart. He knows how much you love him, how much you shine with his beauty. He has a surprise for you. You're going to become pregnant and give birth to a son. He's going to have the name, Jesus. He will be great, the Son of God – one day he'll be king forever.

Mary: But how's that possible? I've never slept with a man!

Gabriel: The power of God will come upon you. The child inside you will be called Holy one, son of God. Nothing is impossible for God.

Mary: [bows down] I am God's servant. Let it happen just as you've said it would.

[GABRIEL and DANIEL leave.]

Daniel: Well, she took that well, didn't she!

Gabriel: Yes, well, God obviously thought she was something special.

Daniel: Didn't you say she was engaged to someone called Joseph?

Gabriel: Yes, Joseph the carpenter. He's a good man.

Daniel: I wonder how he's going to feel about the news?

Gabriel: [looking left] Well, I think we're about to find out.

Scene 4 – Nazareth – Joseph's House

[JOSEPH and MARY enter mid conversation.]

Joseph: I'm sorry, did I hear you correctly? What did you say – you're what?

Mary: I'm pregnant – but it's not what you think.

Joseph: Not what I think? Not what I think? Don't tell me, it's a miracle!

Mary: Actually, yes. An angel visited me and told me I'd be having God's baby. I know it sounds unbelievable.

Joseph: Unbelievable! You can say that again! You must think I'm crazy!

Mary: I don't know what to say … I love you.

Joseph: You don't need to say anything. Love me? I love you. I loved you, anyway. How could you do this to me? I thought we had something special.

Mary: We did, we do. I'd never do anything to hurt you.

Joseph: Look, I can't deal with this right now. I need to be alone. I need some time to think. I'm sorry, but I think you have to go.

[MARY at first reaches out to him, but JOSEPH turns away.]

Joseph: Please go.

[MARY puts her head in her hands and runs off stage.]

Joseph: I can't believe it. I had so much hope for our future. It's all gone now. I can't marry her now, not after what she has done. But I love her. I couldn't bear for her to suffer more than necessary. I'll break off the engagement quietly. People don't need to know.

[JOSEPH sits down on the edge of sofa, with his head in his hands. He mutters – what am I going to do?]

[DANIEL and GABRIEL are standing to the side of the stage.]

Daniel: No, that's not right – it's not her fault – she's not done anything wrong! Can't we do anything?

Gabriel: It's ok, don't panic. He's a good man. He really does love her. He'll come round.

[JOSEPH curls up on the sofa and falls into a fitful sleep.]

Daniel: How will he come round?

Gabriel: I'll pay him a visit.

[GABRIEL walks over to the sleeping JOSEPH and shakes him by the sleeve.]

Gabriel: Joseph, wake up!

[JOSEPH stirs and then sits upright when he sees GABRIEL.]

Joseph: Wh – who are you?

Gabriel: I'm Gabriel. I'm a messenger sent from God. Mind if I sit down?

Joseph: No, of course not.

Gabriel: Thanks. [Sits down next to Joseph]. Joseph, don't break off the engagement. Don't hesitate to get married. Mary's telling you the truth. God's holy spirit has made her pregnant. She's carrying God's special baby – a boy. When he's born, you're to call him Jesus, it means God saves – because he's come to save his people from the all the mess and hurt they get themselves into. That baby boy will be known as Immanuel – which means God is with us. That baby boy will need an earthly dad to look after him, and Mary will need a good, faithful husband. God has a special job for you to do.

Joseph: Wow, I don't know what to say. I can't believe it.

Gabriel: It's true. Please don't be afraid. God can give you the strength you need.

Joseph: But I sent Mary away from me. She looked so devastated.

Gabriel: Well, you know what to do then, don't you?

Joseph: [Getting up off the sofa] Yes, I need to go to her, to tell her that it's all going to be ok. It is going to be ok, isn't it?

Gabriel: Yes. It's all going to be ok. Don't be scared.

Joseph: Right, thanks.

[EXIT Joseph.]

Daniel: Good job, Gabriel!

Gabriel: Thanks! I love my job sometimes!

Scene 5 - Bethlehem

Narrator: So, Joseph and Mary were reconciled. They got married as planned. Months passed, and the day of their son's birth drew near. All was going to plan, until they received some unwanted mail. The Emperor ordered that a census be taken of the whole empire. Everyone had to return to their ancestral hometown to be counted. Joseph was a descendant of King David. This meant he had to make the long trek to Bethlehem, eighty miles away. This was four days travel away. So,

Joseph saddled his donkey, made sure Mary was as comfortable as possible, and they began their long journey.

Gabriel: Four days on a donkey. Wouldn't want to be Mary …

Daniel: or the donkey!

Gabriel: No, maybe not!

Daniel: So, now what happens?

Gabriel: When they get to Bethlehem, they'll need to find somewhere to stay.

Daniel: Aren't there lots of people who will be wanting to stay in Bethlehem? I hope there'll be room for them?

Gabriel: I guess we're going to find out.

Narrator: So, finally, Mary and Joseph arrived in Bethlehem. They were tired, and the baby was due soon, but they didn't know if they'd be able to find somewhere to stay.

[Enter JOSEPH and MARY on the donkey.]

Mary: Joseph, I'm so tired. Can we rest now?

Joseph: It's ok, we've arrived. We'll be able to rest soon. I'm sure we'll be able to find somewhere to stay. We're going to be ok.

Mary: How do you know?

Joseph: Have you forgotten whose baby's inside you?

That baby's going to be the saviour, the King. God will look after us. He is with us.

Mary: I know, I know, I'm just so tired.

Joseph: Look – I have relatives who live here. They'll welcome us for sure. [Knocks on door]

Host: Yes, how can I help?

Joseph: I know it's late, but I'm wondering if you have somewhere my wife and I can stay?

Host: Sorry, who are you?

Joseph: I'm Joseph, son of Jacob, grandson of Matthan. We're family. We've travelled all the way from Nazareth – we've been travelling for four days.

Host: I'm sorry, our guest room's being used at the moment. There's nowhere really for you to stay.

Joseph: But Mary's so tired, our baby's coming soon. Please, is there any way you can help?

Host: Well, let me go and see. Do you mind waiting here?

Joseph: No, of course not.

[HOST goes in the house. MARY holds onto JOSEPH's arm]

Joseph: It's going to be ok, remember that.

Host: Look, there's no space in the guest room.

Joseph: [looks downcast] oh, I see.

Host: But you can stay with my family.

Mary:	Really? Are you sure?
Host:	Of course, we wouldn't turn away our family. Mind you, there isn't much room, – and you'll be with the animals.
Joseph:	Honestly, it's fine. Thank you so much! I told you that it would be ok.
Mary:	You're right, God really is with us.
Host:	Just come round the side, and we'll sort out your donkey.
Daniel:	Well, that's a relief, isn't it!
Gabriel:	I always knew it was going to work out ok.
Daniel:	You are an angel, though – you have an advantage on me!
Gabriel:	That's true.
Daniel:	What are we going to do now?
Gabriel:	Wait, I guess …
Daniel:	What for?
Gabriel:	Jesus to be born, of course!
Daniel:	Of course, sorry. It's a funny place for Jesus to be born, isn't it?
Gabriel:	Why?
Daniel:	It's not very private. When Sammy was born, I went to visit mum in hospital. She had a room to

herself. Mary's not going to have that, will she? [Pause] I hope they're going to be ok.

Gabriel: [puts his arm around DANIEL]. I know. I know. Actually, I think that it's a good place for Jesus to be born. He'll be born among the people – with ordinary people. He hasn't just come for so-called important people, but he's come for ordinary people – to save everybody and nobodies.

Daniel: People like me? He really cares about me?

Gabriel: Exactly!

Daniel: Wow, that's amazing! The prince of heaven, born as an ordinary person. It would have been cool to have Jesus born in my house!

[EXT. noise of baby crying]

Gabriel: You hear that! He's arrived! The prince of heaven has come!

[JOSEPH comes out of the house looking delighted but exhausted]

Joseph: It's a boy!

Gabriel and Daniel: We know!

Joseph: Of course you do – in fact, you knew about him before I did!

Daniel: Can we see him?

Gabriel: Yes, can we?

Joseph: Yes, of course – come in.

[they enter the house to find MARY cradling baby Jesus]

Daniel: [whispering] wow, he's so tiny. Just like baby Sammy when he was born.

Gabriel: It's incredible when you think about it – that's God in the manger.

Mary: And he's my child. My son. [Looks at JOSEPH] – our son.

Daniel: Can I hold him?

Mary: Please do.

Daniel: [takes the baby and rocks him quietly]

Gabriel: Wow, you all look so happy. I'm really sorry, but I've got to go now. I'm off to pass on the news that this special baby has been born.

Daniel: Is it ok if I stay here for a while? It's just that with him I feel everything's going to be ok somehow.

Mary: That's fine by me. Join the family.

Gabriel: Ok, see you all later!

Scene 6 – Field outside Bethlehem

[Three SHEPHERDS asleep in the fields, snoring loudly.]

[Enter GABRIEL]

Gabriel: Ahem! [coughs politely]

[SHEPHERDS still snoring loudly.]

[GABRIEL coughs louder. SHEPHERDS still asleep.]

Gabriel: OI!

[SHEPHERDS grunt and stir, but sleep on.]

Gabriel: There's only one thing for it. A bit of glory's called for. [Claps hands twice.]

[STAGE LIGHTS turned on full.]

[SHEPHERDS wake up with a start, look wildly around, shocked, and scream.]

Shepherds: AAH!

Shepherd 1: Wh – wh – what's going on?

Gabriel: Ahem!

[SHEPHERDS turn and face GABRIEL.]

Shepherds: AAH!

Gabriel: It's ok. Don't be afraid!

Shepherd 1: Don't be afraid? You'd be afraid if you were in our position. We were just minding our own business, watching our flocks by night –

Gabriel: You were asleep actually –

Shepherd 1: - we were resting our eyes, weren't we boys? [other SHEPHERDS nod]

Shepherd 1: umm, well, anyway … we're looking after our sheep and then you appear out of nowhere, scaring us out of our wits with this bright light shining all around –

Gabriel: It's the glory of the Lord, actually. Cool, isn't it?

Shepherd 2: Glory of the … Wh – wh – who are you?

Shepherd 3: And where did you come from?

Shepherd 1: And could you turn the lights down a bit? We're being blinded here!

Gabriel: Yes, yes, ok. [CLICKS FINGERS and LIGHTS dim.] That better? Good. I'm Gabriel, I come from heaven. I'm an angel.

Shepherd 2: Gabriel? An angel? From heaven?

Gabriel: Yes, that's right – do you have to repeat everything I say? Anyway, I've been sent here by the Lord Almighty, creator of the universe, the Alpha and Omega, God himself to bring you a message.

Shepherd 2: Bring us a message? – oh, sorry, repeating you again, aren't I?

Gabriel: That's quite all right. Where was I? Oh yes, I've come to bring you a message. Now where did I put it? [reaches into pocket] Here it is. [Clears throat and reads out.]

"I bring you good news that will cause great joy for all the people. Today in the town of David a Saviour has been born to you; he is the Messiah, the Lord. This will be a sign to you: You will find a baby wrapped in cloths and lying in a manger."

[Folds up paper and puts it back in pocket. Looks at SHEPHERDS who stand with mouths wide open, staring blankly.]

Gabriel: Hello? Did you hear what I just said?

Shepherd 1: A Saviour has been born today, he's the Messiah, the Lord, there's great joy for all people – and you're telling us?

Gabriel: Yes, is that a problem?

Shepherd 2: Have you seen the state of us? Have you smelt us?

Gabriel: Yes, what's wrong?

Shepherd 3: [aside] He's not that bright for an angel, is he? [to GABRIEL] You see, the thing is, we're shepherds. We look after sheep in the fields. We smell like sheep. We're not very important. Are you sure you're in the right place? Did your heavenly sat-nav system go a little wrong?

Gabriel: [aside] He's not very bright for a shepherd, is he? [to SHEPHERDS] No, I've not gone wrong. I meant to come all this way to see you, strange as it seems. I've come to give you the good news.

Shepherd 2: Us?

Gabriel: Yes, that's right. You. This baby that's been born is a very special baby. He's a king. Well, the King of Kings, and he's been born to save the world. He's been born for everybody, including smelly shepherds like your good selves. God Almighty himself wanted you to be the first to know. He happens to have a soft spot for shepherds.

[SHEPHERDS look at each other in amazement.]

Shepherd 1: Can it be true?

Shepherd 2: That a king has been born for us?

Shepherd 3: Us nobodies?

Gabriel: That's the point, actually. You're not nobodies. Not in God's eyes. In fact, nobody's a nobody. Everybody's special to God. That's why this baby's been born.

Shepherd 1: Wow, that's amazing!

Gabriel: Do you want to see him?

Shepherd 2: Can we? But we're not dressed suitably!

Gabriel: It's ok. Don't worry, go just as you are.

Shepherd 3: And we don't have any gifts… What will his parents say?

Gabriel: I really don't think they'll mind. I think they'll be pleased to see you. Go. It's ok. It really is good news for you.

Shepherd 2: Well, what are we waiting for? Let's go to Bethlehem and see this baby!

[SHEPHERDS run out as MUSIC PLAYS "Gloria in excelsis deo."]

Scene 7 - Bethlehem

[SHEPHERDS enter]

Shepherd 3: are we nearly there yet?

Shepherd 1: Yes, yes, nearly.

Shepherd 2: In fact [POINTS TO MARY and JOSEPH] There they are!

Shepherd 3: Wow, a real-life King. And we're going to meet him.

Shepherd 2: Quiet now, he could be asleep.

[SHEPHERDS walk towards family on tiptoes. MARY and JOSEPH sitting down, Jesus in manger. DANIEL is with them. Seeing the shepherds, JOSEPH gets up]

Shepherd 1: Hi, you might think we're crazy, but an angel told us to come here – I think he said his name was Gabriel?

Mary: Yes, we've met him. He said he needed to go somewhere.

Shepherd 1: Yes, he said that a king's been born today and that we'd find him here. Is that him? Can we have a look?

Mary: Be our guest. He's been born for you — for all of us — anyway.

[SHEPHERDS gather around MANGER.]

Shepherd 2: Wow, that's amazing. He's amazing.

Shepherd 1: It's really true.

Shepherd 3: God's in that manger.

[SHEPHERDS bow down in worship.]

[Enter GABRIEL]

Gabriel: [beckons to Daniel] I've got to go now. My work's done. And I think it's time for you to go back home.

Daniel: Yes, you're right. I could stay here forever. I wish I could stay with him forever.

Gabriel: That's the wonderful thing. You can. He is with you. He lives there [points to DANIEL'S heart]. He'll never leave you. He's always with you. That's why he came — to be with us. Nothing can separate you from his love.

[DANIEL and GABRIEL walk off stage]

Scene 8 – Daniel's bedroom

Gabriel: Well, here we are. It's been quite an adventure, hasn't it?

Daniel: You're telling me! Thanks for – well, for everything.

Gabriel: That's no problem. [GABRIEL and DANIEL hug] Things will be ok, you know. You really don't need to be afraid.

Daniel: I know.

Gabriel: See you, Daniel. Good night.

Daniel: [clambers into bed]. Night. And thanks!

[GABRIEL waves and exits stage]

[DANIEL switches off the light]

Narrator: When Daniel woke the next morning, he wasn't sure if he'd been dreaming everything he'd seen and heard. One thing he did know was that he felt different. He didn't feel alone anymore. He knew that whatever happened, somehow, it'd be ok. He knew God cared. He knew that Immanuel – God with us – would never leave him.

PART 2

Proclaiming Good News – the message of Advent and Christmas

Highly Favoured – Luke 1:26-38
(Fourth Sunday of Advent, Year B)

I once heard a story about a cockney from the East End of London who had a real dilemma because he was in love with two very beautiful women. And he couldn't decide. One was called Sharon, and she was blonde and very beautiful, and the other was called Maria, and she was a brunette and also very beautiful. He wasn't a churchgoer, but not knowing whether it was Sharon or Maria, Sharon or Maria, he thought, `Well, I'll go into a church and pray.'

So, he went into a local Catholic church and he knelt down by the altar and he said to the Lord—being a Cockney East Ender, he said: `'oom shall I 'ave?' And he looked up, and he looked at the stained-glass window and he saw in gold letters: *Ave Maria!*[2]

Mary remains a source of great fascination, devotion and inspiration for art and literature, and yet we know so little about her. In a day and age where we love to know everything about everyone, the gospel accounts are so tantalising; frustrating, even. We know very little about these people who, after all, played such a significant part in world history. It's therefore so precious that Luke has recorded these glimpses into the domestic life of Mary and her most famous son, Jesus. In fact, at the beginning of the Gospel Luke writes, "I myself have carefully investigated everything from the beginning, I too decided to write an orderly account" (v3) – it is likely that Luke chapters 1 and 2 were based on Mary's own reminiscences, giving us a wonderful insight into the domestic life of Mary and her relatives and, perhaps most precious of

---

[2] Alpha talk, "How does God guide us?"
http://www.merredinunitingchurch.org/2012/05/24/alpha-talk-how-does-god-guide-us/

all, how she felt at being put at the centre of the great drama of salvation history.

So, what does Luke's Gospel tell us about Mary? The first thing we know is that she lives in Nazareth, a town in Galilee, Northern Israel. Nazareth was a small, insignificant town, with possibly as few as 480 inhabitants. It was an unlikely place for someone so important to live.

The next thing we know is that she is *"a virgin pledged to be married to a man named Joseph, a descendant of David"* (v.27). Jewish tradition of the time is that girls are betrothed at about the age of 12, at which time they would be considered to be married, before being taken home about a year later to the bridegroom's house for normal married life to begin. The fact that Joseph, Mary's fiancé, is a descendent of David is important, because it means that legally Jesus too would be from the line of David.

As we read in verse 26, God has sent Gabriel for this special mission. We have no idea what he looks like, but we do know that when Zechariah sees him, he's terrified, and Mary is greatly troubled. What matters more is that he has an important message to give:

"Greetings, you who are highly favoured! The Lord is with you" (v.28).

There are two key things we need to know about Mary here … she's highly favoured and God's with her. The angel tells her she is "highly favoured", because, though she's an ordinary village girl, God has chosen her for a special blessing. She's an ordinary girl given an extraordinary role in God's work in the world.

The second key thing that we learn from the greeting is that *God is with her*. This is so important. Mary would have a rocky road ahead. The truth of God's faithful and constant presence with her, giving her strength and encouragement, would be something that she would need to hold onto in the weeks, months, and years to come.

How does Mary react to the strange appearance and strange greeting? Unsurprisingly we see she's "greatly troubled" (v.29) and confused, probably wondering what's coming next and why she has this strange visitor. She must be at least a little bit frightened, because Gabriel acts immediately to reassure her, saying, *"Do not be afraid, Mary,"* and repeating that reassurance that she has *"found favour with God"* (v.30).

And then he drops the bombshell in verse 31, *"You will conceive and give birth to a son, and you are to call him Jesus."*

I wonder how much of the angels' message she takes in after that initial phrase, "You will conceive..." (v.31). It is clear that Gabriel is not informing Mary about what will happen once Mary and Joseph come together as man and wife. No, this is different, very different – and Mary knows it. You can tell this by her question, in verse 34 – *"How will this be, since I am a virgin?"* Her question to the angel in the Message translation is even more direct – "But how? I've never slept with a man."

Let's be clear about this. The angel's message to Mary would be an extraordinary and indeed potentially devastating statement to hear. Imagine you're Mary. Men might find this more difficult than women. You're 12. You are pledged to probably a young man called Joseph. You're excited about the forthcoming wedding. Weddings were wonderfully lavish occasions lasting a couple of days and involving the whole community. You've dreamt of this moment since you were a little girl. Now all of these dreams will be taken away from you. Instead of that wonderful wedding feast, there'll be whispers from the community – everyone will know that Mary's having a baby outside of wedlock. Either she and Joseph have been unable to control themselves or worse she's been unfaithful in direct violation of the commandment, "You shall not commit adultery." The penalty for breaking this command is death. If she's worried about how those within the community might react, then this will be nothing compared to the fact she has to face Joseph. He will know that there's been no lack of self-control on his behalf, which will leave only one option – Mary's been unfaithful to him.

This, then, is a big deal for Mary. It's tough to take in. Well might Mary ask how this is going to be possible? Gabriel's response is to tell her,

"The Holy Spirit will come on you, and the power of the Most High will overshadow you. So the holy one to be born will be called the Son of God" (v.35).

One commentator writes,

> This child was not to be born by the normal biological process. He would go through the process of birth, being carried for a full term of pregnancy. Yet he was to differ from all humanity in that he did not have a human father. His conception occurred by the power of the Holy Spirit. This was a miracle in the strictest sense of all: it was an act that only God could bring to pass. God alone can bring something out of nothing: life out of death; fertility from a barren woman; a virgin birth.[3]

The Holy Spirit will be at work in her in a special, wonderful, once off creative way to enable her to have this baby. God will then give her the strength she needs to fulfil the role of being the mother of this child and, presumably, the protection she needs to make sure the baby lives to become all that God has planned. The emphasis here is less on Mary than on God. The angel is saying that this incredible, miraculous work will be God's initiative. God's creative power will make this happen. God is beginning to initiate his great salvation plan. John Nolland writes,

> Luke's emphasis is on the total initiative of God: ... a unique creative act brings into being a child who would otherwise

---

[3] R.C Sproul, *A Walk with God: Luke*, Christian Focus Publications, 2011

never have existed. ... What is emphasised is the total initiative of God in providing the messianic Son.[4]

This leads us to the next key matter – just who is this child?

In verses 31-33 we hear that this baby will be a very special baby – the Son of the Most High, a King who will reign forever. In verse 35 we know that the child will be a *"holy one ... called the Son of God."* These are huge claims to be making about this child – he will be a King, ruling over the whole world. This puts all the kings and those who claim power in any way right in their place. Jesus is the true ruler, which leaves the powers of the world then and now a long way behind. But there's more ... he'll be more than a king. Jesus is identified with God in unique way. The birth of this baby will be massive. He will be both the Son of David, which means he will be the fulfilment of Old Testament prophecy – he is the promised Messiah ... and also the Son of God – this child will have the touch of the divine about him. No wonder the event would go onto split history in two.

The angel Gabriel offers Mary proof of God's miraculous power at work, when he mentions Elizabeth her cousin – *"Even Elizabeth your relative is going to have a child in her old age, and she who was said to be unable to conceive is in her sixth month"* (v.36). There is no natural way that Elizabeth should have been able to conceive, but God's power worked in her. This is a sign for Mary of what she is to experience herself. Gabriel then makes the wonderful statement, *"For no word from God will ever fail" (v.37)* and invites Mary in her own situation to believe in the God of wonders.

Mary has had lots to take in. She is invited to take part in God's amazing salvation plan for the whole world, and her response is wonderful, *"I am the Lord's servant, may your word to*

---

[4] J Nolland, *Word Biblical Commentary: Luke 1-9:20 (Vol 35a)*, Word Books

me be fulfilled" (v.28), or, as the Message translation puts it, "Yes, I see it all now: I'm the Lord's maid, ready to serve. Let it be with me just as you say."

It's worth contrasting Mary's reaction to this unbelievable news to that of Zechariah. It seems that the village teenager is more responsive to promise of God's supernatural power than the Jerusalem priest. Mary has faith that what God has promised will come to pass; that he will work his creative power within her, and that his presence will be with her to help her accomplish all that God has called her to. John Nolland comments, "Mary is here the pattern for Christian faith but also much more: she responds to a call that is unique in human history."

She miraculously conceives, before she then travels to visit the now heavily pregnant Elizabeth whose greeting for her (vv.44-46) is surely wonderful affirmation to her that she wasn't imagining the angel's visit after all – Mary is truly blessed, because she has been chosen to carry a very special baby. Elizabeth is blessed because she is in the presence of the divine and she knows it – even if the divine is in foetal form. No wonder her own miracle baby leaped for joy in the womb!

Mary is blessed, because she has been chosen to carry the very special baby. An ordinary girl has been given the extraordinary privilege of playing a special part in God's salvation plan. God has set her apart for an incredibly particular purpose.

Mary's song at the end of this passage, when she cries out in praise, *"My soul glorifies the Lord and my spirit rejoices in God my Saviour," (vv. 46-47)* focuses on God's choice of an insignificant girl to be his servant and be advanced to the highest honour. We're not going to look at its content in depth this morning, but a glimpse tells us that how God works, "defying human conventions of honour and importance, he is the God of the underdog. Luke will go on to narrate how the ministry of Mary's Son will embody the radical values of the Magnificat"[5]

We may not know as much as we'd like about the woman who carried our Lord and Saviour for nine months and then had the awesome responsibility of bringing him up. All we know is that her name was Mary, she was a virgin, that she'd found favour with God, became pregnant through the power of the Holy Spirit, was obedient and allowed God to work through her in this most extraordinary way. Perhaps, that's all the detail we have, because that's all the detail we need. It tells us of the extraordinary work of an extraordinary God for whom nothing is impossible, who delights in creating life out of seemingly impossible situations.

Our God is the God of the impossible. No word from him ever fails. He brings life out of death, hope out of hopelessness, joy out of sorrow.

This account also tells us that our God works in partnership with us. He could have affected the great salvation plan without involving humans - it might have been an eminently more sensible idea - but he chose not to. He chose to work with us and through us to bring salvation to a broken world. He's still doing that today. Together, God and humanity is the only hope for the world. The question for us is, are we equally open to his power working within us to bring about his plans and purposes for us? Will we respond to God's call on our lives, submitting to the one who rules over all? How do we respond to his claim on us, for absolute allegiance? Will we, like Mary, respond with obedient humility, in words, as Tom Wright notes "which have rung down the years as a model of the human response to God's unexpected vocation"[6]: *"May it be according to your word"* (v.38).

---

[5] R.T. France, *Teach the Text Commentary Series: Luke*, Baker Books
[6] Tom Wright, *Luke for Everyone* (New Testament for Everyone), SPCK

Reluctant Hero – Matthew 1:18-25 (Fourth Sunday of Advent, Year C)

We know the Nativity story so well, don't we? We have heard it and seen interpretations of it so many times. We're so used to it that it no longer seems strange to us. Perhaps it no longer seems as miraculous or even scandalous to us as it once did. We list the events as they are portrayed without even batting an eyelid …

Mary is a virgin in her teens, an angel appears to her to tell her that she's having a baby; but not just any baby – this baby will save people from their sins. Joseph is Mary's fiancé and he hears that Mary's pregnant and has in mind to end the relationship – which is perfectly understandable, considering that the only logical conclusion is that she's been unfaithful to him. However, before he breaks it off, an angel appears to him in a dream and tells him that Mary is telling the truth; that the Holy Spirit is indeed responsible for conceiving the baby growing inside of Mary. Furthermore, that baby will be called Jesus, which means salvation, because he will save the people from their sins. He will also be known by the name Immanuel, which means "God with us." I could go on, but I won't. That's enough to go by for now.

This story is absolutely *incredible*. It's too incredible to be made up. Why would you make up a story that's so scandalous? Because it *was* scandalous, let's not forget it. Joseph, Mary, and Jesus would forever have a stigma attached to them. Who would believe their story that God himself was responsible for the son? People would either assume that Mary and Joseph had been unable to wait until marriage to consummate their relationship or, even worse, that Mary had indulged in an extra-marital affair. Surely these two explanations were more likely than the one Mary and Joseph were giving. Who would believe Joseph and Mary? They knew how unlikely their story would be, so it almost certainly took a great deal of courage to obey God's will in this matter.

We're probably used to seeing Mary's side of the story – we know all about the angel Gabriel and Mary's willingness to obey God, but you could argue that Joseph is definitely the forgotten hero of the nativity story and we hear his side of the story in Matthew. He hears the news about Mary's pregnancy and comes to the conclusion that anyone else would have – that Mary had slept with someone else. According to Jewish law at the time, at the very least he was entitled to break off the betrothal process and technically divorce his bride. We don't know how he responded emotionally to Mary's news. In the excellent BBC Nativity (definitely worth checking out) Joseph starts throwing around the furniture. I think it's entirely plausible that Joseph would have reacted in this way; after all, he was only human and didn't have God's perspective on the issue - not yet, anyway. Mary was asking him to believe the impossible. The alternative to Mary's story must have been unthinkable. Horrible. The Gospel account is light on detail, telling us …

"Because Joseph her husband was faithful to the law, and yet did not want to expose her to public disgrace, he had in mind to divorce her quietly." (v.19)

He was faithful – righteous in some translations, and honourable. He wanted to do what was right, even when so badly hurt, but knew he couldn't marry a woman who had evidently been unfaithful.

At this point, it's a very messy story indeed. And into this mess steps God. God got Mary into this mess and makes sure in his infinite grace that Mary doesn't have to go through it alone.

But after he had considered this, an angel of the Lord appeared to him in a dream and said, "Joseph son of David, do not be afraid to take Mary home as your wife, because what is conceived in her is from the Holy Spirit. She will give birth to a son, and you are to give him the name Jesus, because he will save his people from their sins."

All this took place to fulfil what the Lord had said through the prophet: "The virgin will conceive and give birth to a son, and they will call him Immanuel" (which means "God with us").
(vv. 20-23)

This dream changes nothing – because the baby would never be his, and the whispers would go on, but it also changes everything because he would have known God's presence with him.

Joseph hears the voice and command of God and obeys:

When Joseph woke up, he did what the angel of the Lord had commanded him and took Mary home as his wife. But he did not consummate their marriage until she gave birth to a son. And he gave him the name Jesus.
(vv.24-25)

Because he is righteous and honourable, Joseph stands faithfully by Mary and is a father to Jesus as the baby grows up. In our own time, when fatherlessness has become an epidemic, Joseph's example is a powerful one. Though some still ignore or undermine his part in the nativity, others are beginning to highlight Joseph as a very modern example. Joseph is an example of faithfulness and costly obedience in adversity.

Of course, Joseph may have been completely unperturbed by the turn of events and accepted it all serenely. However, I believe it would have been a struggle; he certainly wouldn't have been in on the plan without God's intervention through the dream; he probably had some sleepless nights and even some nightmares after the dream. But I also believe this with all my heart: God was with them, helping them, inspiring them, keeping them going when the going got tough, every step of the way - not only because of the very precious baby Mary was carrying, but because that's the sort of thing God does. For Joseph this meant he could carry out his duty of being a stepfather to this most precious child because God would be with him, present at all times. Because Immanuel, "God with us" would be with him, helping him, giving him the strength he would need. And what's true for Joseph is true for us too. Immanuel, God with us entered the world two thousand years ago and was born for all of us, to save all of us; and God is still with us now. He will never leave us or forsake us.

On face value, the Christmas story is a messy one, and wouldn't be out of place in some of our soap operas, but at its heart it is a story of great heroism, of people who obey even though they know fully the cost of that obedience, and of great hope, that God himself is present with us in all the mess of our lives and will give us the strength we need to obey him.

Joseph was a hero and a model to all of us of costly obedience. But there's also no doubt that he was only able to be that hero, because of God's intervention and constant presence and inspiration.

May we all know that for ourselves.

A King is Born
(Carols by Candlelight 2013)

It was the most anticipated birth in a long while. The world waited with bated breath for the news – and then, finally we heard. It's a boy! A prince is born! Born to rule. A birth, a boy, a prince, a king. Were some of the headlines that greeted the news of a baby boy to William and Kate on 23 July 2013. I don't know if they'll keep the press cuttings, but there is no escaping who this boy is, and who he will become. He will never be just a normal person. He will carry a nation's expectations and hopes. Who can bear such a load?

We've heard some incredible words tonight. Incredible statements about one person –

"The government will be on his shoulders. And he will be called Wonderful Counsellor, Mighty God, Everlasting Father, Prince of Peace. ... He will reign [forever] ... with justice and righteousness." (Isaiah 9:6-7)

"He will be great and will be called the Son of the Most High. The Lord God will give him the throne of his father David, and he will reign ... forever; his kingdom will never end." (Luke 1:32-33)

He is the Saviour, the Messiah, the Lord.

If we thought we had to wait a while for the latest heir to the throne, this one man's coming had been anticipated for centuries, and when he was born, his birth was heralded, not by the local media, but by angels in heaven who lit the skies with their glory. He was visited by men who travelled thousands of miles to worship him. He was obviously important. You'd expect the whole world to notice. You'd expect him to be born in a palace, in a great city, where great people are born. And yet, we've heard something else perhaps even more extraordinary than these grand statements and claims about his identity – the very same child was born where animals were kept and laid in a manger. Makes a stark difference to a rather plush private hospital. And the angels who lit up the skies with their glory didn't spread the news to important people – they went to shepherds – outcasts in society at the time. Heaven had decreed that these outsiders, these nobodies should be the first to know. Why? Because this was, as the angel said, good news of great joy for **all** the people. While it may be exciting, and I'm really pleased for William and Kate that they can have the joy of parenthood, I'm not sure Prince George's birth is really good news for me. Not really. But this birth is different. The claims about him are too great to be ignored. This baby claims authority over not just a nation, but every nation, over every person who has ever lived, over you and over me. If it's true what the prophets and the angels say, this child changes everything. Suddenly there is a God who has made himself known through this one child. Suddenly there is hope for the world, because this child will return to reign one day with peace and justice. Suddenly there is a God who declares that every child, every man, every woman, matters to him. This means there is hope for you and me. You have infinite worth in God's eyes. You are precious to him.

I wonder what brought you here tonight. Perhaps you came because you fully believe all these statements about this child, Jesus; and you're here to worship. But I wonder if you've come, because it's part of your annual tradition – you enjoy the feeling this season gives you, but it doesn't go much beyond that, and you don't give Jesus much more thought through the rest of the year – or perhaps you've been dragged here by a friend or family member. If that's the case, we're really glad you came, but I wonder, what if these claims are true? What if Jesus is God in human form, born to show you your worth in his eyes? what if God gave himself for you? What if Jesus really is what this Christmas thing is all about? What if he's the greatest gift ever given? How should we respond? Our response to this changes everything. Will you accept this claim, receive this gift? What could you give in response? Perhaps you might be ready to give your heart to Jesus this Christmas. If you are, in a moment we're going to sing "In the bleak midwinter" – you might want to make the final words of this carol your prayer –

"What can I give him, poor as I am?
If I were a shepherd I would bring a lamb,
If I were a wise man I would do my part,
but what I can I give him – give my heart."

Peace (Carols by Candlelight 2014)

Peace – That moment when, as a parent to young children, you finally hear the deep breathing of a sleeping child; that moment when you've got home after a long day's Christmas shopping in the chaos of the city and can relax; the sensation of walking in the countryside having left civilisation behind for just a few hours; that feeling that comes when a situation that has been worrying you for a long period of time gets resolved. Peace. We crave it so much, don't we? We ask our husband, wife, or children for five minutes peace, and we can relate to Mrs Large the elephant in the famous children's story, who takes herself off to the bath seeking refuge from the chaos of family life just for a few moments. Of course, that longed-for five minutes peace never happens. Peace is something we crave and somehow seems unattainable. A dream. Something you pray for when you can't anything think of anything else.

One hundred years ago, there was a moment of peace amidst the violence and chaos of war. On Christmas Day 1914, has been well-documented, enemies left their trenches and ventured into no-mans-land. They buried their dead, sang Christmas carols, exchanged gifts, and played football.

The moment has been immortalised in the Sainsbury's Christmas advert of 2014, but also in Blackadder Goes Forth, when Lieutenant George recalls the moment when "we had that wonderful Christmas truce. Do you remember, sir? We could hear "Silent Night" drifting across the still, clear air of No Man's Land. And then they came, the Germans, emerging out of the freezing night mist, calling to us, and we clambered up over the top and went to meet them." Captain Blackadder replied, "Both sides advanced more during one Christmas than they managed in the next two-and-a-half years of war." Baldrick reminisced, "Do you remember the football match?"

"Remember it?" Blackadder exclaimed, "How could I forget it? I was never offside! I could not believe that decision!"

The Christmas truce of 1914 has been rightly celebrated as a few days of peace in the midst of four awful years of war – the war that was meant to be the war to end all wars. This too, as much as world peace, seems an elusive dream. Conflict carries on, and our dream of peace seems further off than ever.

And yet, we hear that promise once more in our readings this evening. The prophet Isaiah proclaimed the coming of a child who would bring what we all long for … ,

> *"For to us a child is born, to us a son is given, and the government will be on his shoulders. And he will be called Wonderful Counsellor, Mighty God, Everlasting Father, Prince of Peace. Of the greatness of his government and peace there will be no end."* (Isaiah 9:6)

And the angel choir appeared to the shepherds on that hillside outside Bethlehem, singing out, *'Glory to God in the highest heaven, and on earth peace to those on whom his favour rests.* (Luke 2:14)

The message was clear – the baby born in Bethlehem that night came to bring peace. As an adult, he himself said, *"Peace I leave with you; my peace I give you. I do not give to you as the world gives. Do not let your hearts be troubled and do not be afraid."* (John 14:27)

He came to bring peace, and yet wars rage on. Is it just another pipedream, an illusion? What could he possibly mean? How can we possibly find peace? We might find an answer from these words from the early church pioneer St Paul. He proclaimed,

"Christ himself is our peace ... he has made peace between enemies and made us all one family. We were separated as if there were a wall between us, but Christ broke down that wall of hate by giving his own body. ... Christ did all this with his death on the cross. Christ came and preached peace to you who were far away from God, and to those who were near to God. Yes, it is through Christ we all have the right to come to the Father in one Spirit. We are citizens together ... We all belong to God's family"
(Ephesians 2:14-19)

Jesus Christ came to bring peace – firstly between God and us. We are naturally enemies of God. Our deepest inclination is towards rebellion. Being a dad to two lovely, but single-minded girls, I know that obedience is not natural. The instinct is there to push barriers, to do what I want to do, right from the beginning. We cannot help ourselves. We long for peace, but cannot live for peace. We need saving, but cannot save ourselves. The message of Christmas is that Jesus came to deal with this. He came to save us from ourselves. He came to bring us peace between us and God.

He also came to bring peace between ourselves. He broke down the wall of hate. If we are united in Jesus, it doesn't matter if we're black or white, old or young. There can be peace between different people through the power of God. That's why the church at its best is such an incredible thing – a community who are united together, because we all come to God's family.

Finally, he came to bring peace within ourselves. Though the storms will buffet, he can hold us and sustain us through it all. He doesn't take the storms away, but he can be the anchor for our soul.

One day he will return and bring peace forever.

If you long for peace, you can find it, in this holy child of Bethlehem, this prince of peace.

Hope (Carols by Candlelight 2015)

When you hear those familiar words about the word becoming flesh and light shining in the darkness, you may be thinking, so what? What possible light can there be in what's been such a dark year for our world. It's been a year where we've seen an escalation of the refugee crisis encapsulated by that image of that poor boy who'd been washed up on the beach in the summer, terror attacks in Nigeria, Yemen, Kenya, Cameroon, Iraq and Egypt, as well as the US and Paris, and when there's no end in sight to the threat posed to the whole world from Islamic State, it seems that the suffering of countless people seems set to continue. In a world like this where there is so much darkness, the gaiety of Christmas with all the lights and happy music, and talk of joy and hope seem out of place.

In possibly my favourite film, *The Shawshank Redemption*, Andy Dufresne is wrongly imprisoned for the murder of his wife and her lover. He experiences dreadful treatment in prison, He has more right than most to lose hope. And yet, he is the one who brings hope to his fellow inmates; in one classic scene he locks himself in the warden's office to play Mozart over the prison tannoy. Everyone is transfixed - the narrator tells us that, "It was like some beautiful bird flapped into our drab little cage and made these walls dissolve away...and for the briefest of moments – every last man at Shawshank felt free."

For Andy, the music is a reminder that there is always hope, but his best friend Red cannot see the point of having hope in prison: "Hope is a dangerous thing. Drive a man insane. It's got no place here. Better get used to the idea." But when Andy miraculously escapes from Shawshank, he leaves Red with a letter, inviting him to share his hope: "Remember, Red. Hope is a good thing, maybe the best of things, and no good thing ever dies. Your friend, Andy"

On his release from prison, Red is overwhelmed by fear. But that letter from Andy sustains him, reminding him that hope can overcome fear. The final words of the film show how far he has travelled:

> "I find I am so excited I can barely sit still or hold a thought in my head. I think it is the excitement only a free man can feel, a free man at the start of a long journey whose conclusion is uncertain. … I hope I can make it across the border. I hope to see my friend and shake his hand. I hope the Pacific is as blue as it has been in my dreams. … I hope."

"I hope". The very last words of that film. There is so much darkness in *Shawshank*, but it doesn't have the last word. Hope does. Andy Dufresne is right. Hope is the best of things. What a fantastic message to come out one of the most popular films ever made. We all need hope. But, the problem with *Shawshank* is that it doesn't tell you *where* to find hope. And that's what we need to know. When there is so much darkness and tumult around, where do we find hope?

Humanity searches within itself for a solution to the ongoing cycle of violence and evil, and simply cannot find one. We're powerless. Hope remains elusive while we look within ourselves for a solution.

And yet, I believe there is hope, but we have to look elsewhere. We have to look to the story that's unfolded for us in scripture and song this evening, because I believe it's the only hope we have.

Across Europe and in America, the nutcracker soldier is a common Christmas decoration. In the legend of the Nutcracker, brought to life in Tchaikovsky's ballet, a wooden nutcracker soldier comes to life at Christmas time.

What does this magical tale have to do with Christmas? As American author and pastor Dan Schaeffer explains, the idea of wooden soldiers coming to life is an apt picture of what the entrance of God into our world began.

> When God created man and woman in the Garden of Eden, He created them truly human. They did not know evil, and their thoughts and actions were perfect and completely in line with their Creator. They were without sin, without corruption—able to live in God's presence without guilt. However, when sin entered man's nature, our nature, we were no longer truly human the way God created us to be. Sin forever marred His original design, and we became wooden. ... On the outside we looked human, but inside, we became wooden, lifeless, less than truly human. In essence, we traded in our true humanity for a wooden one.[7]

Like the wooden soldier, we have no power of our own to make ourselves human again. But the story we celebrate today, the source of our hope, is that 2,000 years ago, as the angel proclaimed to the shepherds, a Saviour has been born to us. This child was no ordinary child. He was, as we heard in our final reading, the Word made flesh, God in human form. He alone, of every person who has ever lived, was truly human.

As Schaeffer says, "There was no wood in Him, for He was born without the sinful nature we all [share]." He alone lived and loved perfectly. He came to earth to share fully in the fragility and pain of our humanity. While we may identify ourselves with the suffering of the victims of terror attacks by declaring "je suis Charlie or je suis Paris, only Jesus could – and did do that. Jesus came to earth to fully identify with our humanity. This is the miracle of Christmas, and well might we celebrate. But that's not all, there is even more to this miracle. Jesus came, the only truly human baby, to take away our woodenness and breathe his life into us.

"Christ's birth was God's signal that He had come to

---

[7] Dan Schaeffer, *In Search of the Real Spirit of Christmas*, Discovery House Publishers. Kindle Edition.

change our woodenness into true humanity," Schaeffer proclaims. Jesus came, as St John declares, to enable us to become "children of God", to give us a new identity – and then the real miracle begins. Through his power, he has made it possible for us to shed our woodenness and become human, to become more the people who he's made us to be. He's given us the ability, though his power, to choose love rather than hate, to seek forgiveness rather than vengeance, to work for peace rather than pursue conflict, and to experience healing and hope where there has been brokenness and darkness. We see lived out all over the world through the acts of compassion all over the world that are done in Jesus' name, and we don't even need to look that far. In Coventry, thanks to the ministry of the church, the hungry are fed through Foodbanks, the homeless are given shelter from the cold in the winter, and refugees will find a welcome.

It doesn't happen overnight – it takes time, but God can make us real again. I've seen this happen in my own life, and in the life of others as well, who have experienced wholeness and healing through the power of God who is at work in their lives to make them more whole.

The Christmas story we've heard today is one of hope, because God saw our woodenness and hopelessness and stepped in. Jesus became like us 2000 years ago to enable us to become more like him today, to awaken us from our wooden slumber, to enable us to become truly human. We will never be perfect; there will always be much of the wooden about us, but God can bring us to life here and now.

Every Advent I place a wooden soldier is in my living room. The rest of the year it lives on my desk. I see it and remember the true Christmas miracle. I remember that Jesus was born to take away my woodenness and help me become truly human. In this world of tumult and suffering, he is the only hope we have, and the only hope we need.

Do not be afraid
(Carols by Candlelight 2016)

Brexit, the US election, Syria, a refugee crisis that has spread all over Europe, terrorist atrocities. 2016. A year of fear. So much so that xenophobia was announced last month as Dictionary.com's word of the year, defined as "fear or hatred of foreigners, people from different cultures, or strangers."

There is no doubt that fear is a powerful force. In the UK, nearly a fifth of people aged 16 or over showed symptoms of anxiety or depression. Young women between the ages of 16 and 24 are particularly susceptible to anxiety. Fear is a living reality for many people. Fear is powerful, and fear is everywhere.

Fear was also a powerful force in the Nativity narrative too. We dress it up, put tinsel around it, and make it really cute with our nativity plays, but there was fear that first Christmas. First, Mary was afraid when the angel appeared to tell her that she would have God's baby. Joseph too was afraid – afraid, no doubt of what everyone would think when they learned that his fiancée was pregnant outside of wedlock – and that he had nothing to do with it – because no one would surely believe her account that this child was God's baby. Perhaps he was even more afraid of the remote possibility that she was, in fact, telling the truth. What would he do then? And then, the shepherds. Possibly my favourite characters in this wonderful account. They were simply doing their job, minding their own business, going through the monotony of yet another night of guarding their sheep, ready for action in case something out of the ordinary happened. When I say out of the ordinary, I imagine that this would normally take the form of thieves or wild animals that would threaten the flock. They certainly would never have dreamt of anything like the drama that unfolded the night the angels appeared.

First, just one angel came out of nowhere and what's described as the glory of the Lord shone around those shepherds. How did the shepherds react? They were terrified. Scared witless. But it was only an angel making an appearance wasn't it, and we've seen enough of those in nativity plays down the years to know that they're not that scary. Both of my daughters played the parts of angels in their nativity plays last week, and they're not scary!

So, why were the shepherds so scared? Probably because the angel *was* scary; after all, every time angels appeared in the build up to that wonderful Christmas night, they had to begin by saying, "Do not be afraid." Add to this the phenomenon that was "the glory of the Lord" with a light so bright that it illuminated the pitch-black hillside like it was broad daylight and the presence of God that was so tangible, we begin to understand why the shepherds were so scared. The whole experience was terrifying for these men who until now had led uneventful lives. But the angel spoke those most precious words, "Do not be afraid." Then the angel went on to explain why...

"Do not be afraid. I bring you good news of great joy that will be for all the people. This will be a sign to you: You will find a baby wrapped in cloths and lying in a manger."
(Luke 2:11-12)

The shepherds had no reason to be afraid, not just because their lives weren't in danger, but because the angel was the bearer of *"good news of great joy"*. This good news would be for all people. That's everyone – every man and woman, including peasants and shepherds, the unemployed, the retired, farmers, teachers, office workers, shop assistants and even members of the clergy; people like you, people like me. This news was for everyone, and as if to illustrate the point, the first people to know, except for his parents, the carpenter Joseph and peasant girl Mary, were these shepherds.

So, what is the good news? It is of course the birth of a baby, but not just any baby. He is the Saviour, a baby born on behalf of all humanity. The promised King spoken about by the prophets, including the prophet Isaiah one of whose prophecies concerning this King we had read to us earlier. This baby indeed was the promised "Wonderful Counsellor, Mighty God, Everlasting Father, Prince of Peace." And where was this new-born king placed? In a peasant's home, in the animal's feeding trough. It's just a glimpse of the fact that he isn't going to be the type of king that we'd expect. This king would live solely for others. He would give everything so he might serve and save the broken.

There is a wonderful verse in the Scriptures that says, *"There is no fear in love. But perfect love drives out fear"* (1 John 4:18). On that night in Bethlehem, a baby was born. This baby was perfect love in human form and he would drive out all fear. On that night, it wasn't just the shepherds who didn't need to be afraid anymore.

The message of the angel to those shepherds that night resounds throughout the centuries. It is a message for us here today, just as much as it was for them all those years ago.

Do not be afraid, the angel says to *us*.

Do not be afraid, because a baby has been born who would welcome the outcast and fight for the oppressed.

Do not be afraid, because a baby has been born who would fight all the evil we see in the world and he would win.

Do not be afraid, because a baby has been born who would bring great light to a people walking in darkness.

Do not be afraid, because a baby has been born who will rule the world one day in perfect justice and righteousness.

Do not be afraid, because a baby has been born who will ensure that corruption and injustice will be no more.

Do not be afraid, because a baby has been born who has defeated the enemies that terrorise us – sin, sickness, and death.

Do not be afraid, because a baby has been born who stands with us in the darkest places – in the hospital waiting room, or the graveside, or the empty home, or in your loneliness, or in the prison of your infirmity.

Do not be afraid, because a baby has been born for you.

His name is Jesus. He is the Messiah. He is the Lord, and he will cast away all our fear, if we only have faith in him.

Do not be afraid…

God with us (Carols by Candlelight 2017)

2017. A year of terror attacks on our streets and in one of our premier concert venues, targeting those who want to have a bit of fun. A year of mass killings in America. A year of dark deeds being brought to light by courageous women who dared to speak up and say #metoo, illuminating the darkness of sexual abuse. A year where words have been used as weapons by some of the most powerful people in the world. A year where we watched in horror as Grenfell Tower was engulfed in flames, with 71 people losing their lives, and the burnt-out shell of this tower standing as a monument to that horror. For these people and many others, it has been a year of darkness. And it's hard not to feel weary, to have that feeling of dread as we switch on the news as we wonder what else has gone wrong.

I wonder how you will look back on the year, personally? Has it been a year of joy or of heartache? Will you look back as fondly on the year as Prince Harry, excited about his engagement to Meghan Markle? Or do you feel more like the England cricket team, bewildered and wanting to go home? Do you approach Christmas with a heavy heart and glad there's only 8 days to go until it's all over?

I have to say that I've been in that place – when I've not really wanted to celebrate, and I'm a professional Christian – it's my job to lead the celebrations. I felt like a hypocrite, to be honest. I remember feeling alienated from the brightness of the twinkly lights on the estate and the cheeriness of the music on the radio. I remember feeling much more at home in the pitch darkness of the park, which matched the darkness that had descended inside of me.

There are times, aren't there, when we wonder if anything will be able to penetrate the darkness; when hope seems like a distant prospect; when it seems like there's no place for times

121

like Christmas, when people are simply too happy, when we want to wake up on January 6th, or even March 6th when it'll all be over. After all, Christmas is all about the children; it's for those for whom life is hunky dory, who have good reasons to celebrate isn't it?

Actually, Christmas is, as the angel said to the rather bewildered shepherds, "Good news of great joy that is for **all people**." (Luke 2:10) All people everywhere. An extraordinary statement.

Which means this is good news for each of us here. It's good news for old and young, rich, and poor, those who are sick and suffering as well as those who are healthy and happy. It's good news for those for whom life is tough.

I believe that Christmas is of special relevance to those who are struggling, for those who traditionally feel excluded at this time of year; for those for whom darkness is a reality.

Our reading from Isaiah states,
"The people walking in darkness have seen a great light;
on those living in the land of deep darkness a light has dawned"
(Isaiah 9:2).

And in John we hear,
"The light shines in the darkness, and the darkness has not overcome it. The true light that gives light to everyone was coming into the world"
(John 1:4-5).

Jesus came as the light of the world, to shine on those who dwell in darkness.

The darkness may be bereavement, sickness, loneliness, family discord, depression, but into this darkness, God speaks and says, I am there with you, holding your hand, breaking into your darkness. My light can shine through every dark situation in your life.

Do you ever wonder where the fascination with lights that shine in the darkness at Christmas time came from? It came from the belief at the heart of Christmas, that the world's hope comes from outside of it. The light shines in the darkness, Isaiah proclaims, and the source of that light is God – in the same way that the source of the light that shines on earth is the sun.

Hope isn't something that we create or make happen; no, hope is something that has been done for us. God saw the darkness, and he brought Jesus into the world, to be God with us, the light of the world.

The message of Christmas once you strip away the trees and tinsel is that God saw the darkness and despair that so many of us live in, and he did something about it. He sent a child to be born for us. This child was God in human form. He was the source of all light and life and he made his dwelling among us. He knows what it is to experience all the highs and lows of life, laughter and weeping, joy and sorrow. This means God knows our thoughts. He feels our pain with us, and he understands it even more than we do ourselves. He longs for us to share our pain with him, to allow him to carry our burdens. Many of us go through life confused and restless. Jesus is the promised prince of peace and wonderful counsellor. One of the names given to him hundreds of years before his birth was Immanuel, God with us. He came to be God with us, not just during the Christmas season, but every day of the year. Because of Christmas, we know that we are not alone. Christmas is all about this incredible truth of what God has done for us, and whatever we're going through in life, the truth of this will never change.

As Dan Schaeffer writes,

The Christmas spirit can seem beyond our grasp. But if the real Christmas spirit is connected to something God has done for us, then we can still enter into it, even when family ties are weak or severed. For unlike fractured family relationships, Immanuel—God with us—is not isolated from us. Immanuel goes looking for us. He looks for us everywhere. ...

The true celebration of Christmas, then, is the understanding that because Jesus is Immanuel, God with us, He is the answer to our deepest loneliness. Whatever we may be feeling, the truth is that we are never alone. That is God's promise. The last earthly words of Immanuel were, "and surely, I am with you always, to the very end of the age"

"We are no longer alone; God is with us," wrote Dietrich Bonhoeffer. "We are no longer homeless; a bit of the eternal home itself has moved into us. Therefore, we adults can rejoice deeply within our hearts under the Christmas tree, perhaps more than the children are able. We know that God's goodness will once again draw near." ... When we feel alone or abandoned, we can cling to this precious truth.[8]

Jesus came to light up our darkness, to bring hope where there is hopelessness. He came to bring comfort. He came for you and me, our saviour, our redeemer. Because of this, whatever we're going through, we have every cause to celebrate. Wish it could be Christmas every day? It can be, because of the reality of Immanuel, God with us, who promises to be with us every single day of the year, to bring hope for life, not just for Christmas.

I pray that the truth of God's love; the reality of the hope of Christmas would shine in our hearts today and every day.

---

[8] Dan Schaeffer, *In Search of the Real Spirit of Christmas,* Discovery House Publishers. Kindle Edition.

Follow the Star
(Carols by Candlelight 2018)

How far would you go to fulfil an ambition? I have a confession and I know that it may diminish me in some of your eyes. About a month ago I went to London - on Black Friday, of all days – just to have Cliff Richard sign a CD. Here's the photographic evidence that I was there. I apologise that I may have lost all respect you may have once have had for me.

What may surprise you even more is that I wasn't the only one. There were hundreds of us who queued up for their 30 seconds with Cliff and his scribble on a CD. In fact, if you think I was a little crazy - and my wife Liz thinks I'm barking mad - I met someone there who'd flown especially from Germany - and she told me another woman had come from - wait for it - Singapore. So, there you go!

What have you woken up at ridiculous times to get - tickets to Wembley for the 87 cup final? A concert with your favourite band? A bargain purchase?

Have you ever, like me, travelled a rather long way for something that after all would only last a minute or two?

We do that sort of thing, like climb mountains just for the view from the top, drive hours to catch that sunset -

What is worth that sort of devotion?

Two thousand years ago, stargazers saw something in the sky that arrested their attention. They saw a star that they'd not seen before. It heralded something extraordinary. A seismic, even cosmic event. The birth of a King. Not just any King, but a King whose birth had implications that transcended time and space.

They set out with one purpose – to worship the new-born king. Though we don't know details, these mysterious magi came from the east, possibly ancient Persia, modern-day Iran, a journey of over 500 miles through inhospitable and uninhabitable landscapes. On foot. There would have been no hotels or creature comforts. The return journey would have taken months – and if you take into consideration the time they would have needed to prepare, you're looking at six months away from home. Why? The answer was simply that these mysterious magi from the east had come to worship the one who was born king of the Jews. Then, when they finally arrived at Bethlehem, via Jerusalem, they saw the child and Mary and bowed down to worship him. The gifts they gave him have become legendary - *gold, frankincense, and myrrh.*

You have to admire their tenacity. I wonder how much time they actually spent at their destination before making their long journey home? Not long, I imagine. But their journey no doubt must have been worth it, because they came face to face with the child Jesus. They came to worship him. They gave him their valuable treasures, but you know what, I don't think their treasures were the most precious gifts they gave him. The most precious gift they gave Jesus was their devotion and their worship. They put everything else aside that they might bow down at his feet.

I wonder what brought you here this evening. How far have you travelled? Last year I spoke with someone who had come here all the way from the other side of Birmingham to be at this service, and my parents have travelled from near Oxford, so they probably win the long-distance award. Most of us have come from the estate, we've not travelled far. But I guess each of us is on a spiritual journey. You may be here because you this has been part of your Christmas tradition, and it's lovely to welcome you here. You may be here, because you, like the magi, are on the journey of a lifetime. You're seeking something, perhaps you're wondering where this spiritual journey leads – you might be wondering whether there's something in this time of Christmas, when the light pierces the darkness and we're reminded of the most extraordinary gift, when we're encouraged to give of the best to each other. We have to be honest and say that so often Christmas leaves us flat, not quite satisfied. No gifts that we receive will truly satisfy. Not even family time will be perfect – there'll be something that won't quite be right, someone will possibly say the wrong thing, get the wrong present, the food might burn – and even if it all comes off perfectly, how long will the Christmassy feeling that we crave really last?

Simon Guillebaud recounts the following story:

A platoon of soldiers was marching through the blistering heat of the Egyptian desert during the Second World War in desperate pursuit of water. The guide was confident of where to find it, but suddenly one of the troops spotted a beautiful desert lake several miles away. It was undeniable. So despite the guide's pleading, they hurried off course towards the beautiful water. Sadly as they approached, the Lake grew smaller and smaller until it disappeared in the sand. It had been appearance without reality. They had chased a mirage, and we only know about this because one of the soldiers recorded in his journal in his dying hours.[9]

So many things present themselves as being like this mirage – they look so beautiful, promise so much, yet in reality they are mirages. They will never truly satisfy. The magi are mysterious, even eccentric figures, but they were onto something – there's only one thing, one person who can truly satisfy. Jesus alone, the reason for this season, can fulfil our deepest longings

2,000 years ago, many different people were invited to meet the baby Jesus – ragged shepherds, mysterious wise men, - it doesn't matter who you are, where you've come from, like the magi, you can follow the star, come as you are, imperfections and all.

---

[9] Simon Guillebaud, *Choose Life: 365 Readings for Radical Disciples*, Monarch

As the Archbishops of York and Canterbury said as they launched the Church of England #FollowtheStar Christmas campaign in 2018, "come just as you are to take the life-changing Christmas journey. Wherever you are this Christmas, you are invited to follow the star and to be with Jesus. You are welcome. You are deeply known and truly loved."[10]

> A young man once tried a number of things in a succession of desperate searches for fulfilment: excessive pleasures, false religions, philosophy, dissipation and distractions, causing his mum significant heartache, but they didn't satisfy. He was desperate and cried out to God, "How long, O Lord, how long?" God answered that cry and his life changed forever. He was called Augustine, and is now considered one of the key Saints in the church's history. He wrote a prayer to God, "You have made us for yourself, O Lord, and our hearts are restless until they find their rest in you.[11]

Each Christmas we are reminded of God's longing to surprise us with his gift of joy, love and new life. It's the greatest present we can receive and share with others!

Take this journey and discover one who has been waiting for you all your life. Take this journey and find the end to your life's searching. Take this journey and find the rest you need. With the wise men, follow the star. As the choir will sing in a moment, I'd like to invite you to go to Bethlehem –

> "The Kings are travelling, travel with them!
> The star of mercy, the star of grace,
> Shall lead your heart to its resting place.
> Gold, incense, myrrh you cannot bring;
> Offer thy heart to the infant King."

---

[10] https://www.archbishopofcanterbury.org/news/latest-news/archbishop-justin-welby-switches-christmas-lights-lambeth-palace
[11] Christian History Institute, "Our hearts are restless", https://www.christianhistoryinstitute.org/incontext/article/augustine/

The government will be on his shoulders (Carols by Candlelight 2019)

"For to us a child is born, to us a son is given, and the government will be on his shoulders."
(Isaiah 9:6-7)

These words send a thrill of hope, and relief through me. What we need just now, as much as any time I've ever known, is someone to shoulder the burden, someone who can pick up the multiple problems we have in our nation and carry them for us. And, no matter what he promised in the wake of his election victory, Boris Johnson make various pledges of how his government will lead this nation into a time of healing. It sounds good, but it isn't something he could deliver - neither could Jeremy Corbyn or Jo Swinson for that matter. No manifesto, no matter how brilliantly put together or delivered can make that kind of difference. They cannot bear that weight. I remember the wave of hope that spread around the world at the election of Barack Obama when he was elected. Of course, no matter how brilliant he was, he couldn't match the expectation thrust upon him – he was unable to solve the world's problems – no one could. Except one. *"For to us a child is born, to us a son is given, and the government will be on his shoulders."*

Who is this figure that the prophet speaks about? None other than the one whose birth we've been remembering tonight. The baby who the shepherds were told would be found wrapped in cloths and lying in a manger. We think of Christmas as a comforting time - rightly so, because it reminds us of the fact that God thought us of such worth that though he was and is the creator of the heavens and earth he became human, a tiny, fragile baby. In that manger was a baby who may have had tiny fingers but he has the whole world in his hands. What an incredible thing to do, to step into the mess of our human frailty, to show such love and demonstrate our worth to him.

So, there is great comfort in Christmas, but there is challenge too, because the temptation for us is to leave him there in the manger, to tidy him away with our nativity sets on the twelfth night, until we get him out and dust him down in December next year. But that was never the intention. The baby grew up. He grew up to be the one on whose shoulders the government would rest forever. He was born to rule, to become King. King, not just of Israel, but King of the whole earth. The true king of Europe, the true King of our United Kingdom, of England. The true King of me. Of you. This doesn't mean he is another sort of politician on whom everybody can pin their hopes and who will let them down. His rule and reign is one of justice and peace. He has different ways, a different manifesto. A manifesto that proclaims good news for those who are poor, abandoned, forsaken. A manifesto that proclaims healing and hope for the broken and hurting. And, unlike many manifestos that, despite the noblest of intentions, remain unfulfilled, this man grows up to practice exactly what he preaches – he puts God's kingdom into practice and shows us what it looks like for God to become King.

As the then Bishop of Durham, N.T. Wright, exhorted in his sermon at the Midnight Eucharist in 2008,

> Watch, in the gospels, as the Wonderful Counsellor goes to work, dealing with individuals but also confronting the systems which had enslaved them, and upsetting the slave masters. Watch as the Mighty God strides through Galilee feeding the hungry, healing the sick, rescuing people and restoring creation itself. Look on in awe as the Everlasting Father is seen mirrored in the incarnate Son, giving himself totally to his beloved world. And … watch as Jesus, from his earliest beginnings with a price on his head through to his riding the donkey into Jerusalem, shows what it looks like when the Prince of Peace is on the

move. He comes to get God's kingdom off the ground – or perhaps we should say, precisely *onto* the ground, the real life of real people. And that involves taking upon himself the full force of the world's cruel systems, the political and economic enslavement from which we still suffer, so that the power of evil can be broken and something new may take its place. That was true at Jesus' birth, as it was true at his death.[12]

Jesus lives out his manifesto. But he doesn't leave it there. He invites you and I to respond, he invites us to join in with his mission, to sign up to his manifesto of radical, self-giving love. Love your neighbour, he calls us. Love your enemy, love yourself, do all of this rooted in the knowledge that you yourself are loved beyond your imagination, so much so that this child, in that manger, grew up to live and die for you.

Sign up to his party. Live out his values and ways. Protect the vulnerable, protest against injustice, ensure that Kingdom values are lived out in our homes, workplaces, communities, and churches, to be those who are determined to love, love the worthy and unworthy alike, and to be the first to forgive, even if the people voted Leave – or Remain, Conservative or Labour or Brexit Party.

But, we cry, that's impossible. How could we do such a thing, live in such a way? It's possible thanks to the one on whose shoulders the government shall rest.

N.T. Wright illustrates the difference Jesus makes:
He offers to heal and renew human beings, calling us as he called his first followers to the dangerous, difficult but glorious task of working as his agents, growing the kingdom as we say, making it happen for real people in the real world.

With the story of the Christ-child in our hearts, and the Spirit of Jesus giving us energy and direction, we are called to be kingdom-bringers in whatever sphere we can. We have to

---

[12] N.T. Wright, "The Government Shall Be Upon His Shoulders," 2008 https://ntwrightpage.com/2016/03/30/the-government-shall-be-upon-his-shoulders/

think globally and act locally, campaigning for the big issues like debt remission and climate change, and working on the local issues like housing, asylum, unemployment and loneliness. Bit by bit, the kingdom of God can grow and grow, as justice and peace spreads throughout the world, through the work of those who follow Jesus, the King. ...

This kingdom gets to work when we stop, and pause, and look in wonder once more at the baby lying in the manger, and like Mary ponder in our hearts what it all means. Only through deep devotion to the child who is born to us, the son who is given to us, can we make sure that the government really is upon his shoulders, and so prevent our good intentions being misdirected to serve our own ends, real or imagined.

The thing is, we need a Saviour. No human politicians can solve the massive mess that we find ourselves in. As Vaclav Havel, the first president of the Czech Republic, said, "Pursuit of the good life will not help humanity save itself, nor is democracy alone enough. A turning to and seeing of ... God is needed." The human race constantly forgets, he added, that "he is not God."

Turn to the Christ-child. It begins with worship. Praise him tonight. Give thanks that he stepped in and became human. Gather in worship and wonder at the side of the manger. But then do the challenging thing. Allow him to grow up in your life. Acknowledge him as God and let him have control of your life. Allow him to open your eyes afresh to his ways of doing things. Ask for his help to love in the way he calls you to, and to live out his manifesto. Allow him to give you a vision of how things could be. Celebrate the fact that the government is on his shoulders.

Comfort and Joy
(Carols by Candlelight 2020)

In the words of one of our carols this evening, the story we've heard unfolding through those readings and beautiful carols are tidings of comfort and joy.

News of comfort and joy.

Comfort and joy? Really? What does that mean? How, after all, can we find comfort and joy from this story? How can there be comfort and joy after a year like this one? After that news announcement last night – and today's newspapers declaring, "Christmas is cancelled." Comfort and joy is exactly what we need right now.

I like the word comfort, don't you? especially when paired up with other words ...

We all like our creature comforts that make us feel at home, some of us may have a comfort blanket, after a year like this one, all of us have indulged in a bit of comfort food this year – Friday night chocolate in our home, accompanied by a little bit of port or a glass of red – rioja if anyone's wondering what to buy me this Christmas; we've definitely been pushed out of our comfort zone as we've grappled with technology or home schooled our children, had to cope with working from home or connected with neighbours who until that point had been strangers to us; we'll also have been binge watching TV series to give us comfort in these challenging times. For me, as I was getting increasingly anxious in the build-up to the US Presidential election and in the weeks afterwards, I've drawn comfort from The West Wing.

We've drawn comfort from music that we love - Christmas tunes entered the charts this year earlier than ever before, and Mariah Carey finally got her number 1 26 years after the release of "All I want for Christmas is you". But it's not just Christmas music - in difficult times we listen to familiar tunes that move us or help us in some way. Around this time of year, one of my go-to pieces of music is Handel's Messiah- telling the story in music of how Jesus and why he matters. What I particularly love about the work is that it begins so beautifully with the words, "Comfort, comfort my people." When telling the story of Jesus Christ, his life, death and resurrection, Handel could have started anywhere, with any message, but he began with a message of comfort. Why? I believe that the good news we celebrate at Jesus is at its heart one of comfort. God sent his son to rescue and save people who are struggling, who need to be comforted. And we probably all find ourselves in this boat this year.

As J John recently wrote,

> The messiness of Bethlehem is no accident. It's in the messes that God is most able to help us. 'I didn't come to call the righteous,' Jesus said, 'I came to call the sinners.' He might as well have said, 'I didn't come to call those who have got it right, I came to call those who are in a mess.' Those whose Christmases – and lives – are in disrepair are those most likely to listen to God.[13]

One of our Bible readings begins …
"The people walking in darkness have seen a great light;
on those living in the land of deep darkness a light has dawned."
(Isaiah 9:2)

It is those who are in darkness who are able to see the great light. The light is dawning on those who live in this deep darkness. The darkness may be bereavement, sickness,

---

[13] J John, "The Christmas Fantasy", *Premier Christianity* (2015) https://www.premierchristianity.com/home/the-christmas-fantasy/803.article

loneliness, family discord, depression, but into this darkness, God speaks and says, I can break in. My light can shine through every dark situation in your life.

The message of Christmas once you strip away the trees and tinsel is that God saw the darkness and despair that so many of us live in, and he did something about it. He sent a child to be born for us. This child was God in human form. He was the source of all light and life and he made his dwelling among us. He knows what it is to experience all the highs and lows of life, laughter and weeping, joy and sorrow. This means God knows our thoughts. He feels our pain with us, and he understands it even more than we do ourselves. He longs for us to share our pain with him, to allow him to carry our burdens. Many of us go through life confused and restless. Jesus is the promised prince of peace and wonderful counsellor. One of the names given to him hundreds of years before his birth was Immanuel, God with us. He came to be God with us, not just during the Christmas season, but every day of the year. Because of Christmas, we know that we are not alone. Christmas is all about this incredible truth of what God has done for us, and whatever we're going through in life, the truth of this will never change.

This is why we can take comfort this Christmas, because God has come to be with us right in the midst of our mess and he hasn't left us on our own.

We are no longer alone; God is with us,' wrote Dietrich Bonhoeffer. 'We are no longer homeless; a bit of the eternal home itself has moved into us. Therefore, we adults can rejoice deeply within our hearts under the Christmas tree, perhaps more than the children are able. We know that God's goodness will once again draw near.' ... When we feel alone or abandoned, we can cling to this precious truth.[14]

---

[14] Schaeffer, *In Search of the Real Spirit of Christmas*, Discovery House Publishers. Kindle Edition.

Jesus came to light up our darkness, to bring hope where there is hopelessness. He came to bring comfort. He came for you and me, our saviour, our redeemer. Because of this, whatever we're going through, we have every cause to celebrate.

These, then, are genuinely tidings of comfort. But they're also tidings of joy.

The angel said to the shepherds, "I bring you good news of great joy that will be for all people" (Luke 2:10) Great joy? How is that possible?

Joy is something we link inextricably to happiness, but it's so much deeper than that. Happiness is so dependent on our circumstances. On Wednesday I was happy one moment and then it all changed because Liverpool scored in the last minute against Spurs and we lost the match. I wonder if you can relate to this!

You're happy one moment and then you find yourself swept away by a sudden sad memory or thought.

No, happiness is so fleeting. Joy is different. Kay Warren is someone who has known significant hardship in her life - her son took his own life when he was in his 20s. She released a revised version of her book, *Choose Joy – because happiness is not enough* in light of his death. She says, "The only thing that would allow me to survive the loss of my son was what I knew and believed about God . . . and joy."

In *Choose Joy,* Warren gives us this definition of joy –

> Joy is the settled assurance that God is in control of all the details of my life, the quiet confidence that ultimately everything is going to be all right, and the determined choice to praise God in all things.[15]

---

[15] Kay Warren, *Choose Joy – because happiness isn't enough*, Fleming H. Revell (2020 edition)

If we've learned anything this year, it's how out of control we are. How many of us have lost count of the plans we've needed to revise because something has been cancelled or postponed? We are not in control. But I believe that God is in control, somehow, even if I can't see or understand it. Everything is going to be alright ultimately, because Jesus was born to deal with all the mess of our world, the sin and suffering, and although we celebrate his coming as a baby, he grew up to become a man whose death and resurrection mean the prospect of life forever and that light will overcome the darkness – and he's coming back one day and when he does all will be well.

Kay Warren also writes, "Joy is rooted in gratitude. You cannot have a joyful heart without having a grateful heart."

We have a decision to make this Christmas. Are we going to bemoan all that we're missing out on – and I'm sure we could make a fairly long list, or are we going to choose to be thankful for the things we have? Because, my bet is that this list will be even longer. This year I've been grateful for the beauty around us in the changing seasons, often right on our doorstep, I've been grateful for my family, for the gift of technology, enabling us to stay connected, for my church family and their emails and encouragement of me and each other. I won't go on. But I also know I have to choose gratitude. To make that conscious choice to look for the positives.

As Warren exhorts,

If we are going to experience joy in this lifetime, there's only one possible way: We will have to choose it. We will have to choose it in spite of unbelievable circumstances. We will have to choose it in the middle of a situation that seems too hard to bear. We will have to choose it even if our worst nightmare comes true. This isn't what we want to hear. We keep trying to line up all the little ducks in a row, to smooth out the rough spots, and to shore up all the wobbly places, still convinced that if we get our act together, we finish the huge project, our health clears up, we get a raise, or we can just get things right, we can finally be joyful.

Christmas is not cancelled. This Christmas we can truly celebrate, because God has come to bring us comfort. I want to encourage you, whatever your circumstances, to choose joy. God is with you, he will never leave you, and all will be well – and all manner of things shall be well.

At the Heart of Christmas
(Carols by Candlelight 2021)

It was the most holy of nights. One that the shepherds would certainly never forget. I imagine Mary and Joseph wouldn't forget that night either, the night when their firstborn was born. Although the conception was extraordinary, the birth was most likely like any other. The pain and sweat, the exhaustion, but determination of a young woman to bring a new life into the world. The brief silence, broken by the crying of a child, messy, helpless, but perfect in the eyes of his parents who were, if they're anything like me filled with tears themselves, and above all, dearly loved.

There would have been other children born that night – possibly even in Bethlehem, equally dearly loved. But no other birth had been quite so highly anticipated, spoken about by prophets hundreds of years previously:

> *"To us a child is born, to us a Son is given. and the government will be on his shoulders. And he will be called Wonderful Counsellor, Mighty God, Everlasting Father, Prince of Peace."* (Isaiah 9:6)

No other child's birth had been heralded by angels, terrifying those unsuspecting shepherds when the glory of God lit up the hillside around them, and bewildering them with the extraordinary tidings of

> *"Good news that will cause great joy for all the people. Today in the town of David a Saviour has been born to you; he is the Messiah, the Lord. This will be a sign to you: You will find a baby wrapped in cloths and lying in a manger."* (Luke 2:10-12)

No other birth announcement had accompanying it a host of angels appearing, *"praising God and saying, "Glory to God in the*

highest heaven, and on earth peace to those on whom his favour rests."
(v.13-14).

Although it was a birth like any other, He was a child like no other, who grew up to be a man like no other. As the angel made clear – to those shepherds, as well as to Mary and Joseph a few months earlier, and as God made clear through the prophet Isaiah, this child was born for a reason. ...

He was born to be a King ...
"The Lord God will give him the throne ... and he will reign ... for ever; his kingdom will never end." (Matthew 1:32)
"The government will be on his shoulders" (Isaiah 9:6)

He was born to be a Saviour. The name he was given by the angel, Jesus, means "God saves." He was born to *"save his people from their sins"* (Matthew 1:21).

His was a birth like no other. Unique in human history. Every other birth, even if it hasn't been planned, has been conceived through human action. Not this one. Although she responded in obedience when others might have run a mile, Mary didn't choose to be the mother of Jesus. Joseph wouldn't have gone ahead with the marriage were it not for the intervention of the angel who appeared in a dream reassuring him that she was telling the truth and that this was God's plan. The shepherds would have carried on with their normal business of watching over their flocks, if the angel hadn't appeared.

Why, you might be wondering, am I labouring the point? What am I getting at? It's just struck me just how passive all the people were in the unfolding of this plan. It was all God. All his action. All his doing. There was nothing they did about it. They were recipients, called to cooperate and respond.

Why is this so important? Because I feel it goes against the grain of what seems to be our focus this time of year. Our focus is on what we give – how good we can make others feel, whether through the gifts we have carefully chosen or made, or through the charitable donations we've made. It's wonderful to feel that we're making a difference, it's wonderful making people happy. This is why Charles Dickens' *A Christmas Carol* is so popular. There are 19 film versions of this story, none better in my opinion than A Muppet's Christmas Carol, and with good reason – it's so wonderful to see the transformation of Ebenezer Scrooge from miser and meanie to a man characterised by generosity, at the heart of the party. I love that story, and watch it most years if possible, because the message at the heart is a good one – it is truly more blessed to give than receive.

The problem is when we allow Christmas to become the celebration of how good we are, how much we give. The shocking reality of Christmas is that we are completely in debt, and there is nothing we can ever do to deserve the gift God lavished on us.

How easy do you find that to hear? How much do you, like me, want to justify yourself and list all the good things you have done; demonstrating somehow that you are deserving of this act of love?

Receiving something we don't feel we deserve makes us uncomfortable, doesn't it? And yet we're all in this position this year, thanks to the COVID vaccine programme. Many of us have now been triple-jabbed. And what an amazing thing the vaccine programme has been. Although things feel a little bit wobbly with the advent of omicron, the vaccine has given us the path towards some semblance of normality. Without it, goodness knows where we'd be as a country. I suspect we'd be in a bit of a pickle. Medical science has given us this incredible gift of the vaccine – and very few of us have done anything to deserve this gift, apart from the few who have worked in medical science, or been part of the army of those who have been vaccinating others. The rest of us are grateful recipients of this gift – and we've not had to pay a thing.

How have you felt receiving this vaccine? After my first COVID jab in May I walked out of the medical centre feeling a little bit teary – My overwhelming feeling was gratitude and a sense of wanting to be able to give something back. But we can't, not really. We can't earn the vaccine. It's been given freely to us – yes, our taxes have paid for it – but you can't put a price on what the vaccine has done for us – all thanks to those who've worked on the vaccines on our behalf.

At Christmas, God in his abundant generosity gave a broken, dying and hurting world the purest gift of life, light and love in the form of Jesus, not because we deserved or earned it, but because he is love, because he is generous and merciful. God "comes to us, blesses us with a gift, and calls us to see ourselves as we are — empty-handed recipients of a gracious God who, rather than leave us to our own devices, gave us a baby."[16]

So, this Christmas, I invite you to humble yourself, set pride aside and receive this most wonderful gift. Like Mary, like Joseph, we can't give anything in response, except our openness, our willingness to receive this gift.

Receive this gift for what it is – an undeserved gift from someone who loves us overwhelmingly and completely. Receive his incredible, undying love for you. And if you really want to give something back, then we could do no better than this – in the words of the beautiful "In the bleak midwinter", "What can I give him, poor as I am … what I can I give him, give my heart."

Give your heart to him today. You won't regret it.

---

[16] William Willimon, "The God we hardly knew", in *Watch for the Light: Readings for Advent and Christmas*, Orbis Books

Life after Christmas (Luke 2:21-40)

So, the decorations have gone up in the loft, the tree's been put away, or in our case, chopped into bits and put into the bin; Christmas is over. I don't know about you, but I feel a little sad – everything looks bare. The streets no longer look inviting as all the lights have been put away. We're left to reflect on a Christmas time that perhaps wasn't quite all it could have been, or if it was, left with normal life that seems a little bit duller – and there's the issue of the credit card bill that's going to come any time now. ... All in all, we feel a little flat. Blue Monday is coming – 21st January, which is claimed to be the most depressing day of the year. All the wonder of Christmas seems a long time ago. What do we do after Christmas?

I wonder how it was for Mary and Joseph once things had calmed down a bit, after the excitement of the night their special baby was born. They were probably still with Joseph's family they'd been staying with since arriving in Bethlehem a couple of weeks before. They were probably still marvelling at and mulling over the visit from the shepherds with all they'd had to report about the angel's message. Perhaps those words were ringing in their ears ... "A Saviour has been born to you, he is Christ the Lord" – did it seem real to them as Mary was trying to recover from the birth, as they were both no doubt dealing with the exhaustion, the sleepless nights, feeding the baby and dealing with whatever passed for nappies in those days, and that sense that every first-time parent experiences of wondering what on earth has hit them? Did they look at the baby Jesus as they were cradling him in their arms and wonder if it had all been a dream? What was it like for them after Christmas, and how can we learn from them? Let's look together at Luke 2:21-40.

Firstly, as we see in verse 21, as devout Jews, they had duties to complete – at home, on the eighth day, they circumcised the baby and gave him the name Jesus, given to him by the angel before he conceived. Mary and Joseph were ensuring that the angel's instructions were faithfully carried out.

A month later, they travelled the short distance to the temple at Jerusalem, about 5 miles away, for Mary to purify herself *"as required by the Law of Moses"* (v.22), and for Jesus to be "presented to the Lord". Right from the beginning, Jesus' life is characterised by total obedience to God. They go to the temple where they offer "a sacrifice in keeping with what is said in the Law of the Lord: "a pair of doves or two young pigeons." This comes from Leviticus 12, which outlines the purification rites that were to be performed after the birth of a child. Normally a lamb and a dove should be brought as the expected offering, but if a couple were poor, they could bring two doves or two young pigeons. We have an insight here into Mary and Joseph's financial position – they were clearly poor. It's a wonder and a reminder that our Saviour chose to be born into the most ordinary of families. So, there was probably nothing exceptional about this little family on that day, no one would have taken much notice of them – except one did. His name was Simeon, and he was on the lookout, he was attuned to find the exceptional in the ordinary.

We know little about Simeon – except that he was righteous and devout (v.25) and, like many, *"waiting for the consolation of Israel."* He, like Anna, was a loyal patriotic Jew who knew from the Scriptures that God had promised a better future for his people.

Significantly, we learn that Simeon was not acting purely under his own guidance, that what happened next was not a chance encounter. There was another agent at work … look at verses 25-27, *"the Holy Spirit was on him. It had been revealed to him by the Holy Spirit that he would not die before he had seen the Lord's Messiah. Moved by the Spirit, he went into the temple courts."*

The Holy Spirit, who we've seen already in Luke's Gospel has had a significant role to play in the unfolding of this salvation story – he was present in the conception of Jesus, filled Elizabeth when Mary visited her, filled Zechariah and inspired him to utter the wonderful song of praise at the end of Luke 1, now compelled Simeon, gave him revelation that God was on the move and would bring Israel their long-awaited Messiah within his lifetime, now moved his feet into the temple, because now was the time, the waiting was over. So, Simeon entered the temple courts – either the Court of Gentiles or Court of Women, because that's as far as Mary could go into the temple. There he saw this couple that perhaps everyone else had overlooked…. He was given eyes to see that behind the ordinary, something extraordinary was happening.

> *"When the parents brought in the child Jesus to do for him what the custom of the Law required, Simeon took him in his arms and praised God"* (v.28)

It's a rather beautiful moment, isn't it? An eruption of joy as this old man takes this baby – not much bigger than George – in his arms and sings this song to God.

> *"Sovereign Lord, as you have promised,*
> *you may now dismiss your servant in peace.*
> *For my eyes have seen your salvation, …*
> *which you have prepared in the sight of all nations:*
> *a light for revelation to the Gentiles,*
> *and the glory of your people Israel."*
> (vv.29-32)

It's a song of praise to the God who keeps his promises. Simeon had been told by God that he would see that Messiah face to face, but we're not told how long he had held onto this promise. Had there been moments of excitement followed by disappointment before? How many babies had he held in his arms as he did with Jesus here in v. 28, how many times did he catch his breath, look down and wonder if *this* child might be the one? How many times was he filled with disappointment as he realised he'd have to wait just a little bit longer?

We don't know. But we do know that as he held this baby, he knew that God had kept his promise. I think that Luke really wants us to grasp this point as he also introduces us to Anna, an elderly widow, aged 84, who was devoted to God, and saw Mary, Joseph, and Jesus, and gave thanks to God for the arrival of this baby, that redemption was on its way, embodied in the baby Jesus.

God is faithful and keeps his promises. I wonder if we've received a promise of God that we're finding it hard to cling to? Well, keep strong, keep firm. God is faithful and keeps his promises. God had given the world the Saviour that it so badly needed. And of all the promises that God has ever made, this is the one that really counts. And because we know he kept his promise then, he will do again. Perhaps this, as we begin life after Christmas, is something we can cling to. Our God is faithful. The Saviour we've sung about in carols, he really came, and he's with us now. The promise of Christmas, that there is good news for all people, is still good news for you and me today. The angel's message that we needn't be afraid rings as true today, for a Saviour has been born for us. Jesus is still Immanuel, God with us, in the messy aftermath of Christmas just as much as he was in the midst of the wonder and excitement of the Christmas celebrations. Truths like this can encourage us and keep us going through difficult times. I love that line in verse 33 that they Mary and Joseph *"marvelled about what was said about Jesus"*. We put them on pedestals, but forget that they were just kids and needed encouragement just as much as we would have. Perhaps Simeon's words were what they needed to get them through what would be some dark and scary times in the not too distant future – they might give them the strength and reassurance to keep going after the visit of the magi in Matthew 2, when they were rudely awoken by the angel in the middle of the night and sent to flee to Egypt because Jesus' life was in danger. Perhaps these words kept them going through their years as refugees, far from home.

We're coming to the end, but before I close, I want to reflect for a moment about the particular Words spoken over Jesus by Simeon and their relevance for us as we live life after Christmas. Extraordinary as it must seem, the hope of the world rested on the shoulders of a tiny Jewish baby – God's salvation was seen in this six-week-old baby born to parents who couldn't afford to pay the proper price of the sacrifice. We have here a snapshot of God's ways – he is beginning to inaugurate his upside-down Kingdom. As St Paul would later say, *"God chose the foolish things of the world to shame the wise; God chose the weak things of the world to shame the strong"* (1 Corinthians 1:27). Ordinary people like you and me get a place as royalty in God's Kingdom. We are of infinite worth to him, whatever others may say about us. But there is an even bigger truth that Simeon's words -

> *"My eyes have seen your salvation, which you have prepared in the sight of all nations: a light for revelation to the Gentiles and the glory of your people Israel."*

This is first indication in the Gospel that God's plan for salvation, though rooted in the Jewish people and their Jewish Messiah, would embrace the whole world, including gentiles, traditionally seen as outsiders. Now, thanks to Jesus, no one is an outsider. God's salvation reaches all. No one is beyond the bounds of his love. It doesn't matter who we are or what we've done. God's love is for us.

Finally, though, we're given a glimpse of the cost involved in this plan of salvation. Let's look at verses 34 and 35.

"Then Simeon blessed them and said to Mary, his mother: "This child is destined to cause the falling and rising of many in Israel, and to be a sign that will be spoken against, so that the thoughts of many hearts will be revealed. And a sword will pierce your own soul too."

These words to Mary would have been sobering. Firstly, it's clear that Jesus will be a controversial figure. He would be a sign that will be spoken against, there will be those who will seek to oppose him. His ministry will be uncomfortable and divisive. As he provokes opposition, people will be obliged to take sides. Even today we see this is true. It's impossible to be neutral about Jesus. Not if you take seriously what he is said about him and what he will claim for himself. You can't be neutral about someone who claims he is Lord of Lords and King of Kings.

Simeon speaks of the *"sword that will pierce your own soul too"* – here, we see that the shadow of the cross looms over Mary. Simeon's words looking forward to her experience of bereavement. It will be costly for her to have the Messiah as her son.

Following Jesus is costly. He is Lord and as such, claims our total allegiance. Jesus doesn't promise to shield us from this cost, from the potential heartache that following him may bring, but he does promise that in the end, our faithful following of him will be well worth it. He is, after all, the one who came before us, lived the life of total obedience that we cannot come near to living. He was the one who bore the ultimate cost for our disobedience on the cross, taking all of our sin upon himself. He bore the separation from God so that we wouldn't have to. We can have a relationship with God, filled with the Spirit, thanks to Jesus. By rising from the dead, He gave us hope that withstands death. The main point about life after Christmas is that there'd be no reason to celebrate Christmas without Easter. He came to be our Saviour. He came to be his mother's Saviour too – as is put in "Mary did you know", "the child that you delivered would soon deliver you". Mary herself, though she experienced confusion and bewilderment and rejection at times in Jesus' ministry, and the heartache of the cross, would be witness to the resurrection and was present on the day of Pentecost, filled with the Holy Spirit. And now, she's united with her Lord in heaven. Stay faithful, it'll be costly, but it'll be well worth it.

So, after Christmas, let's cling to the truth that God is faithful and keeps his promises. And let's stay faithful to him, it will be well, well worth it. As we live life after Christmas, cling to God's promises, and be shored up by hope. We have seen the Lord's salvation, and one day he will return to complete the job he's started. One day he will return and he will bring us to live the perfect lives with him in a world where there will be no more pain, no more sadness, no more suffering and no more tears.

In the meantime, we wait. We wait for Jesus to return. We wait for our fervent prayers to be answered, but we do so knowing that God is faithful and keeps his promises.

PART 3
Responding to the Story

Was it badly planned?

Dear God and Lord almighty, creator of it all,
I have a few questions about the Christmas festival.
Each year we remember these events so long ago –
We sing and tell the story – but there's lots I still don't know.
You see, the problem is, I don't quite understand
Why it happened the way it did – was it badly planned?

Your mother was a peasant girl, so fragile and so young,
Her fiancé was a hero, reluctant and unsung.
How did you know they'd bear the load,
that they wouldn't crack?
Why take such a massive risk – there would be no way back.
Why involve us humans – we could have made a mess
Of this great salvation plan – it could have cost you less.

You could have come in splendour more fitting for a king
– anything would have been better
for the Lord of everything –
So, why choose rejection? why choose the manger?
Why those first visitors – it couldn't get much stranger
than these smelly shepherds. Could you really trust them?
They were outcasts, after all, not creme-de la creme.

Surely such a baby deserves a V.I.P.
Not riff-raff or outsiders, not people just like me.
Or was that just the point? Do we need to know
We're infinitely precious – is that what Christmas shows?
Was the Christ-child born for all? Is it really true
that Immanuel – God-with-us – is the perfect gift from you?

And can I really come to you in all my sin and shame?
Do you take me as I am, give me a brand new name?

"Beloved" now, and "chosen", "forgiven" and set free -
Accepted by the Saviour, who lived and died for me.
I simply cannot take it in, not even a tiny part
But I thank you, God, for Christmas,
from the bottom of my heart.

No Room

Was there really no room for you that night?
Didn't they know who you were
And the precious baby you carried?
Was there really no room at all?

Was there really no room for you that night?
Not even a space on the floor?
Was there a better place to lay your head
than with the animals and the straw?

Was there really no room for you that night?
Why didn't you kick up a fuss?
After all, you were a VIP –
and your baby, the most important of all.

Was there really no room for you that night?
I can't imagine how that must have felt …
The sting of rejection, the shutting of doors
The shrugs and the shakes and the tuts.

Was there really no room for you that night?
Is there really no room for your Son?
What kind of God goes to that sort of length
Only to hear us say 'No.'

Was there really no room for you that night?
Lord, there's not enough room in me.
Please knock on my door, make yourself at home
And make me the way I should be.

Wonder

This is a series of poems written for an "Alternative Carol Service" we did at church in 2019. See Appendix Two for a suggested service outline.

The Reason for Wonder

All I see is the mess that surrounds me –
All I hear is the noise and the clamour –
All I feel is the pressure upon me –
demands and deadlines compete for my time.
Together, they threaten to engulf me,
To steal away peace and trouble my dreams.
I try to hide it, but cannot fight it
The despair that's rising and growing in me.

Is this all there is? Can't we hope for more?
Still yourself long enough, look and you'll see
Clues of a deeper truth – reality.
It's in the embrace of your faithful friend,
It's in the laughter of the innocent,
It's in the tears of solidarity,
It's in starlit skies and autumn colours
These signposts that invite you to wonder.

Wonder at love and joy and at beauty
Where do they come from and what do they mean?
Could they be chance, with no rhyme or reason,
Or are they signs of purpose and meaning?
In the midst of the fog of confusion
Come and explore for a moment with me
The true story of love beyond measure
The reason for hope, for life, and wonder.

*   *   *

In the beginning was ... Hope.

In the beginning was ... Hope.
Light. A pinprick. Dazzling bright.
Piercing the darkness.
Because in the beginning you were right here with me
You saw every moment, you saw and stepped in.
When I was flailing and failing,
To us a child is born ... to me. Even me.
When I'm confused and confounded
To us a son is given ... to me, even me.
When I've lost my way and fear for the future
The government will be on his shoulders
You bear the weight that I cannot carry.
When I need advice, when I pour our my heart
He will be called wonderful counsellor ... you counsel me.
When surrounded by what seems to be impossible
He will be called mighty God ... I remember you're far stronger
than me.
When I need to be held,
He will be called Everlasting Father – I can be
When I need to be quieted - *He will be called Prince of peace.*
Because of you, I can be still.
Your light shines bright and hope dawns in my heart.

*   *   *

Bigger than the Universe

I've held a new-born child.
Utterly vulnerable, dependent on me.

I've known that feeling of awe and wonder
As the heart beat nineteen to the dozen in that tiny chest.
I've felt the grip of those minute fingers,
surprised by the strength within.
I've looked into those eyes with tears in my own
And felt the love surging through my being.
This life I held was a miracle.
How much more the One who was born that night?
The One wrapped in cloths and placed in a manger
Just like any other child, yet unlike anyone who has ever
lived.
This child whose tiny fingers gripped his mothers'
Was the one who has the world in his hands.
This child whose heart beat in that tiny chest
Was the one who gives life to everyone.
This tiny child was bigger than the universe.

*   *   *

Born to Save

This tiny child was born to save
That's what the angels said.
That's what they sang
as their praises lit the midnight sky.
Born to save
Not just the sorted,
the good
the great
the worthy
But born to save
Ordinary people
Born to save me with my mess and my muddle,
my doubts, insecurities, flailing and failings.

No wonder the shepherds ran to see
If it was real
Or was it fake news,
Too good to be true.
They ran with hope and returned with joy
It was true.
This tiny child was born
For me.
For you.

*　　*　　*

Come and See

Come and see what love has done.
Come and see your worth to him.
Come and see and wonder
Wonder at the One who saw
our brokenness
our mess.
And stepped in.
Jesus.
Immanuel
God with us
Wonder at his name.
He wove together a beautiful tapestry
From the broken threads of our humanity.
He brought hope, healing, redemption,
This redeeming work goes on.
It began that night,
That night of wonder.
As I gaze upon
that scene of infinite love
in infinitesimal form
I am filled with wonder.

One heart, one life, one love

Written for The Alternative Carol Service, themed around the Church of England theme for 2021, "At the heart of Christmas" and inspired by the wonderful, spine-tingling prologue to John's Gospel. See Appendix Three for a suggested service outline

In the beginning was the Word, and the Word was with God, and the Word was God. [2] He was with God in the beginning. [3] Through him all things were made; without him nothing was made that has been made. [4] In him was life, and that life was the light of all mankind. [5] The light shines in the darkness, and the darkness has not overcome it.

[9] The true light that gives light to everyone was coming into the world. [10] He was in the world, and though the world was made through him, the world did not recognise him. [11] He came to that which was his own, but his own did not receive him. [12] Yet to all who did receive him, to those who believed in his name, he gave the right to become children of God – [13] children born not of natural descent, nor of human decision or a husband's will, but born of God.

[14] The Word became flesh and made his dwelling among us. We have seen his glory, the glory of the one and only Son, who came from the Father, full of grace and truth.

(John 1:1-4, 9-14)

In the beginning beat a heart
And the heart was life and the heart was love,
There was just love at the beginning
And love had to create
So create Love did - and with a Word
brought it all into being -

Countless stars, planets - a universe so vast -
beyond our imagination and comprehension.
and among the innumerable worlds
chose just one where life would thrive
This planet - earth - came alive
An explosion of colour
a cacophony of sound
every detail, from the tiniest creature
to the vastest mountain plain
displaying his glory, showing his heart.
But that's not all - that wasn't enough
For the heart beat for more -
Love had to relate as well as create -
So, saving the best for last,
the heart reached from within
and made creatures who, at their best,
would be just like him …
Able to love, bring life,
whose hearts would beat just like his.
Together their hearts would beat as one
One heart, one life, one love.

And yet, these hearts had to choose to love
But so often, instead, these hearts chose hate
or simply chose love of self over love of others
and so, these hearts changed
Warm hearts grew cold
Soft hearts grew hard
Glad hearts became sad
And whole hearts broke
Lost hope.

But the heart that began it all
kept on beating,
kept sustaining

kept life-giving
and reached within once more
One Pure heart
became flesh and blood,
One of us.
Through this love heart
cold hearts warmed
hard hearts softened
sad hearts gladdened
and broken hearts healed
They could become new.
Hope could return.

And hope lives on
This heart keeps beating
keeps sustaining
keeps life-giving
In you and me
in anyone who will receive him
His heart can become our heart
His love our love
Our heart could beat just like his.
Together our hearts would beat as one
One heart, one life, one love.

PART 4
Reflecting on the Story

An Advent and Christmas Devotional

For a couple of years, I posted daily Tweet-length Bible passages accompanied by short reflections. If Here are the daily readings for Advent and Christmas. If you wish you could use this as a short devotional for during this season.

Day 1 – 1st December

"I will lead the blind by a road they do not know, by paths they have not known I will guide them. I will turn the darkness before them into light, the rough places into level ground. These are the things I will do, and I will not forsake them."
(Isaiah 42:16)

This month many churches will welcome visitors to celebrate Christmas with them, praying that hearts respond to the truth of God's love for them. These verses remind us that while we're called to proclaim the Gospel faithfully, it's the Lord who leads people on the way of faith.

Day 2 – 2nd December

Rise up, O Lord! Why sleep? Rouse yourself! Don't reject us forever. Why do you hide your face and forget our grief and oppression? We're brought down to the dust; our bodies cling to the ground. Rise up and help us; rescue us because of your unfailing love.
(Psalm 44:23-26)

I'm trying to resist the urge to launch into full Christmas mode. Much as I love the sparkle and cheesy music, the older

I get the more I realise I need Advent. I need space to acknowledge that all is not yet as it should be, to cry out to one who hears and will one day rescue.

Day 3 – 3rd December

"Hallelujah! For our Lord God Almighty reigns. Let's rejoice and be glad and give him glory! For the Lamb's wedding's come, and his bride's made herself ready. Bright, clean fine linen, was given her to wear." (fine linen is the righteous deeds of the saints.)
(Revelation 19:6-8)

In Advent we pray for the renewing of God's church. Too often division and hatred mar the image of Jesus in us we're called to show to a broken and hurting world. But we're not left without hope - Jesus is at work in his church. He will restore his people; his light will shine.

Day 4 – 4th December

The Lord who created and formed you says, "Fear not, for I've redeemed you; I've called you by name; you're mine. When you go through deep waters, through rivers of difficulty, I'll be with you, you won't drown. For I'm the Lord your God, your Saviour."
(Isaiah 43:1-3)

In #Advent we're invited to cling to hope in the face of very real darkness and difficulty. It may be derided as "pie in the sky" but it's founded on a person who overcame the ultimate darkness of death and destruction for us. Holding us tightly he says, "Fear not, you're mine."

Day 5 – 5th December

"Look! God's home is now among his people. He will live with them, and they will be his people. God himself will be with them. He'll wipe every tear from their eyes. There'll be no more death, sorrow, crying or pain. All these things are gone forever."
(Revelation 21:3-4)

In Advent we look forward to when all suffering will end. Our present reality is merely temporary. God will return and make all things right, making his home with us. We know this because his promise is founded in that birth in Bethlehem. God is the ultimate promise keeper.

Day 6 – 6th December

As the deer pants for streams of water, so my soul pants for you, my God. My soul thirsts for God, for the living God. When can I go and meet with God?
(Psalm 42:1-2)

Advent reminds us of our hunger and thirst, our very real spiritual poverty. There's only one who can truly satisfy. Jesus promised, "God blesses those who are poor and realise their need for him, for the Kingdom of Heaven is theirs" (Matthew 5:3). Let's make space to meet with him

Day 7 – 7th December

"The Lamb's servants will see his face, and his name will be on their foreheads. There will be no more night. They will not need the light of a lamp or the light of the sun, for the Lord God will give them light. And they will reign for ever and ever."
(Revelation 22:4-5)

The darkness that surrounds us, though at times overwhelming, is temporary. In Advent we recall the coming of the Light of the World in our midst. He conquered the darkness. The Lamb has won. He will return to be reunited with his people, those he has claimed for himself.

Day 8 - 8th December

The Spirit and the bride say, "Come!" Let the one who hears say, "Come!" Let anyone who's thirsty come. Let anyone who desires drink freely from the water of life. He who testifies to these things says, "Yes, I am coming soon." Amen. Come, Lord Jesus.
(Revelation 22:17,20-21)

Jesus offers an open invitation- if you thirst for more than this world could ever offer you, come. Come as you are. Drink the water of life. Whether you've walked with the Lord for a long time; whether you used to but do no longer; whether you've never met with him: simply come.

Day 9 – 9th December

Oh, that you would rend the heavens and come down, that the mountains would tremble before you! As when fire sets twigs ablaze and causes water to boil, come down to make your name known to your enemies and cause the nations to quake before you!
(Isaiah 64:1-2)

Do you pray with this kind of passion? Do you have the same longing for God to move in our land? The absolute, sometimes brutal honesty of the Scriptures can put us to shame. God, give us a true passion for you and your glory. May our hearts break for the things that break yours.

Day 10 – 10th December

We always thank God for all of you and continually mention you in our prayers. We remember before our God and Father your work produced by faith, your labour prompted by love, and your endurance inspired by hope in our Lord Jesus Christ."
(1 Thessalonians 1:2-3)

St. Paul speaks of faith, hope, and love as being key foundations to the life of a Christian. They should be the source of all we do. Our faith inspires our work, our love motivates us to work hard, and our hope in Christ enables us to keep going in the face of difficulty.

Day 11 – 11th December

"Listen to me, I have cared for you since you were born. Yes, I carried you before you were born. I will be your God throughout your lifetime— until your hair is white with age. I made you, and I will care for you. I will carry you along and save you."
(Isaiah 46:3-4)

I think this is one of my favourite promises in the Bible. We cannot outlive God's love and care for us. We're precious to our creator God. We have no "best before" date in his eyes. He's sustained us from the moment we were conceived and will do so until we draw our last breath.

Day 12 – 12th December

The Lord your God is with you, He is mighty to save. He will take great delight in you; he will quiet you with his love; He will rejoice over you with singing.
(Zephaniah 3:17)

This is a verse that I've committed to memory since I was a teenager. There's so much rich, life giving truth in these few words. Our God is the mighty warrior King and he delights, rejoices, dances even, over us. He is with us. His love for us is unquenchable and inexhaustible.

Day 13 – 13th December

Yes, my soul, find rest in God; my hope comes from him. He's my protector and deliverer, I won't be shaken. My salvation and honour depend on God, my mighty rock, my refuge. Trust in him at all times, O people; pour out your heart to him; God's our refuge.
(Psalm 62:5-8)

Our dependency needs to be on God. Humans are fallible and fragile - the turbulence we often witness in our nation's political life is a stark reminder of this. God alone won't let us down. God alone can deliver us. In God alone is hope found. We can cry out to him.

Day 14 – 14th December

May the Lord make you increase and abound in love for one other and for all, just as ours does for you. May he strengthen your hearts so that you'll be blameless and holy in the presence of our God and Father when our Lord Jesus comes with all his saints.
(1 Thessalonians 3:12-13)

"Love God and love one another" While we may know the heart of Jesus' teaching about how he calls us to live, we find it much harder to love out. Paul's prayer's reassuring - it implies we're not alone in needing help to love but also that this help is available to those who ask.

Day 15 – 15th December

This is what the Lord says— your Redeemer, the Holy One of Israel:
"I am the Lord your God, who teaches you what is best for you, who
directs you in the way you should go."
(Isaiah 48:17)

I love what this verse reveals about God and his relationship
with us - his desire is that we grow to become the Christlike
people he's called us to be and would use our circumstances
to teach and guide us. It's down to us - are we willing to be
led? Are we open to being taught?

Day 16 – 16th December

He made me into a polished arrow. He said to me, "You are my
servant, in whom I'll display my splendour. " But I said, "I've laboured
in vain; I've spent my strength for nothing at all. Yet what is due me is
in the Lord's hand, and my reward is with my God."
(Isaiah 49:2-4)

There are times when work for Jesus is incredibly
discouraging- we work hard and faithfully, we pray for and
share our faith with friends and family, seemingly to no avail.
We may feel like our efforts are wasted and no one notices,
but God sees. God notices. It is not in vain.

Day 17 – 17th December

Let's be sober, wearing the armour of hope and love and helmet of the
hope of salvation. For God chose to save us through Jesus, not to pour
out his anger on us. Jesus died for us so that, whether we're dead or alive
when he returns, we can live with him forever.
(1 Thessalonians 5:8-10)

With just 8 days to go, are you ready? This passage is all about being prepared, not for Christmas but for Jesus' return. Advent invites us to live in such a way that when Jesus comes out of the blue we'll truly joyful. Let's examine our hearts and pray for more of God's grace.

Day 18 – 18th December

The Lord's given me his words of wisdom, so that I know how to comfort the weary. Each morning he wakes me and opens my understanding to his will. As the Lord helps me, I won't be disgraced. Therefore I've set my face like flint; I know I won't be put to shame.
(Isaiah 50:4,7)

Jesus was the fulfilment of Isaiah's prophecies about the "suffering servant". He knew and lived out God's law perfectly and perfectly embodied the wisdom and compassion of God. Extraordinary though it may seem, through the Holy Spirit that same gift of wisdom can be given to us.

Day 19 – 19th December

May God enable you to live a life worthy of his call and give you the power to accomplish all the good things your faith prompts you to do, that the name of Jesus may be glorified in you, and you in him, according to the grace of our God and the Lord Jesus.
(2 Thessalonians 1:11-12)

St Paul rarely prays for a change in circumstances, but rather prays that he or others would be better equipped to respond to their circumstances. We can't often control what happens to us, but we can control the way we react, and ask for God's grace to help us when we need it.

Day 20 – 20th December

Awake, awake, arm of the Lord, clothe yourself with strength! Awake, as in days gone by, as in generations of old? Was it not you who dried up the sea, the waters of the great deep, who made a road in the depths of the sea so that the redeemed might cross over?
(Isaiah 51:9-10)

I love the often brutal honesty of the Bible, when prophets, priests and poets alike cry out in bewilderment, "God, what on earth are you doing? Wake up! Do something about .... soon!" Oh for that kind of honesty in my prayer life and in the worshipping life of our churches.

Day 21 – 21st December

Brothers and sisters, pray for us that the message of the Lord glorified everywhere, just as it is among you.
(2 Thessalonians 3:1)

May I ask you to pray with me for all those given the awesome privilege and responsibility of preaching the Gospel over this Christmas period. May good news be shared, may many encounter the Word Made Flesh, Immanuel himself for the first time and above all may God be glorified.

Day 22 – 22nd December

Burst into songs of joy together, you ruins of Jerusalem, for the Lord has comforted his people, he has redeemed Jerusalem. The Lord will lay bare his holy arm in the sight of all the nations, and all the ends of the earth will see the salvation of our God.
(Isaiah 52:9-10)

There is hope for those who feel ruined. A Saviour's come for you. He is the mighty redeemer. Immanuel, God's with you. You will not be left where you are. He'll hold you and comfort you. He will enable you to sing songs of joy once more, and the whole earth will see his glory.

Day 23 – 23rd December

"I, Jesus, am the Root and the Offspring of David, and the bright Morning Star." The Spirit and the bride say, "Come!" And let the one who hears say, "Come!" Let the one who is thirsty come; and let the one who wishes take the free gift of the water of life."
(Revelation 22:16-17)

Jesus is the promised Saviour one in whom all hunger is satisfied, in whom all hope finds fulfilment. His light alone penetrates the darkness. He is the only gift that we truly need. #FollowTheStar, come and taste and see. He waits for you and knocks at the door of your heart.

Day 24 – Christmas Eve

"In the tender compassion of our God the dawn from on high shall break upon us, To shine on those who dwell in darkness and the shadow of death, and to guide our feet into the way of peace."
(Luke 1.78-79)

In his tender mercy God himself came to a world lost and languishing in darkness to shine his light. To a world tearing itself apart he came to be our peace. To those under the shadow of death he came to be life. Light, peace and life will have the final word. All because of Him.

Day 25 – Christmas Day

While they were there, the time came for her to deliver her child. And she gave birth to her firstborn, a son. She wrapped him in cloths and placed him in a manger, because there was no guest room available for them.
(Luke 2:6-7)

All ages & stages,
all welcome, all can worship
Beauty in the messiness, light puncturing the darkness;
Peace found amidst the chaos, hope within your reach.
Want to find him? Simply still yourself
Listen & you'll hear
Love's heartbeat made incarnate
closer than you think.

Day 26 – 26th December

"Do not be afraid. I bring you good news that will cause great joy for all the people. Today in the town of David a Saviour's been born to you; he's the Messiah, the Lord. This will be a sign to you: You'll find a baby wrapped in cloths and lying in a manger."
(Luke 2:10-12)

Christmas is universal good news, because every soul needs a Saviour, from presidents and monarchs to those who are in prison. We're all in the same boat. The journey of faith begins when we lay our pride at the feet of the one whose days began in the manger.

Day 27 – 27th December

To all who received him, who believed in his name, he gave the right to become children of God. The Word became flesh and made his dwelling among us. We have seen his glory, the glory of the one and only Son, who came from the Father, full of grace and truth.

Though I don't normally mark saints days, today being St John the evangelist gives me the excuse of quoting the glorious passage above. Here we're reminded of why the coming of Jesus is such good news. God became human, one of us. Celebrate it, savour it, wonder, and worship!

Day 28 – 28th December

In him was life, and that life was the light of all mankind. The light shines in the darkness, and the darkness has not overcome it.
(John 1:4-5)

There is no circumstance so hopeless, no pain so unbearable, no hurt so acute that God's presence cannot reach and light up. Jesus is the light of the world. He came to be Immanuel in the mess and pain of our lives. He can reignite the flame of hope within you.

Day 29 – 29th December

"See, I will create new heavens and a new earth. The former things will not be remembered, nor will they come to mind.
But be glad and rejoice forever in what I will create,
for I will create Jerusalem to be a delight
and its people a joy."
(Isaiah 65:17-18)

This seems a distant dream, but we can trust that God will one day bring this promise to fulfilment, because of his first coming among us. Immanuel began the earth's journey towards full redemption. What we see around us isn't the final story. There'll be a new dawn, a new day.

Day 30 – 30th December

"Rejoice greatly with Jerusalem and be glad for her, all you who love and mourn over her." For God says: "I'll extend peace to her like a river, and the wealth of nations like a flooding stream; you'll nurse and be carried on her arm and dandled on her knees."
(Isaiah 66:10-12)

At the end of Isaiah comes the wonderful promise of hope and restoration for ruined and exiled Jerusalem. This broken people would be the source of hope for the whole world.

This promise was fulfilled when our Saviour Jesus (let's not whitewash him) came - Gods gift to the world.

Day 31 – New Year's Eve

The Word became human and made his home among us. He was full of unfailing love and faithfulness. And we have seen his glory, the glory of the Father's one and only Son.
(John 1:14)

New Year brings mixed emotions as we reflect on the year past and wonder what lies ahead of us. However you feel may you be consoled and encouraged by the stupendous reality that in Jesus God made his home with you. He inhabits every moment. You'll never be alone.

Day 32 – New Year's Day

One thing I ask from the Lord, this only do I seek: that I may dwell in the house of the Lord all the days of my life, to gaze on the beauty of the Lord and to seek him in his temple.
(Psalm 27:4)

This is, I admit, less true than I'd like it to be, although it's also truer than ever before. How good to know that God's presence dwells within me & his beauty's all around. May I ever be more aware of this, discerning his fingerprints in my every day.

Day 33 – 2ⁿᵈ January

Peter said, "Jesus is 'the stone you builders rejected, which has become the cornerstone.' Salvation is found in no one else, for there is no other name under heaven given to mankind by which we must be saved."
(Acts 4:11-12)

Why is Christmas worth celebrating? Because our prayers are answered - God sent a desperate world the Saviour we all need. Jesus is the only Saviour given to the world. He is the Saviour of all people everywhere, even of those who reject him. No one and nothing else can save.

Day 34 – 3ʳᵈ January

You must have the same attitude that Christ Jesus had. Though he was God, he did not think of equality with God as something to cling to. Instead, he gave up his divine privileges; he took the humble position of a slave and was born as a human being.
(Philippians 2:5-7)

As Christmas passes, it's so tempting to move on and forget just how wonderful it is- Jesus, God himself, became human, forsaking the glory of heaven. In the words of the old hymn, "May I never lose the wonder" of this mystery. May I take that wonder with me throughout the year.

Day 35 – 4ᵗʰ January

Jesus came into the world to save sinners— of whom I'm the worst. But God had mercy on me so that Jesus could demonstrate his great patience with even the worst sinners. Then others will realize that they, too, can believe in him and receive eternal life.
(1 Timothy 1:15-16)

Why was Christmas necessary? Because of this. A world above all needed saving from sin. God in his great mercy sent Jesus as the solution to this greatest problem. Each of us, even the very worst, the most broken, can believe and receive eternal life. There is no greater gift.

Day 36 – 5th January

"For God so loved the world that he gave his one and only Son, that whoever believes in him shall not perish but have eternal life. For God did not send his Son into the world to condemn the world, but to save the world through him."
(John 3:16-17)

Christmas is all about love. God's saving love for us. Don't ever doubt your worth to him. He loved us so much that his one and only Son became flesh to bring us life forever. If you remember one thing from these reflections, remember this- you're loved more than you know.

Day 37 – 6th January

When they saw the star, they were overjoyed. On coming to the house, they saw the child with his mother Mary, and they bowed down and worshipped him. Then they opened their treasures and presented him with gifts of gold, frankincense and myrrh.
(Matthew 2:10-11)

Though the magi's strange gifts might have been valuable, by far and away the most precious gift they gave Jesus was their devotion and worship; the gift of themselves. You may not feel you have much to offer Jesus; simply come as you are, give him your heart.

Appendix One – Remembering with Mary (Outline of a Service during Christmas Season)[17]

Opening prayer

Carol – O come, all ye faithful

Reading – Luke 2:19

Reflection – How it all began

Reading: Matthew 1:18-25

A candle is lit

Prayer – for those who are finding life difficult; for those who feel misunderstood; for those whose marriages are under strain

Carol – O little town of Bethlehem

Reflection – Arriving in Bethlehem

Reading – Hebrews 12:1-2, 12-13

A candle is lit

Prayer – for our own spiritual journeys; for our own

---

[17] This outline is taken from Ruth Burgess *Hay & Stardust: Resources for Christmas to Candlemas,* Wild Goose Publications

ministries of hospitality, that we may be more welcoming of people, more welcoming of Christ.

Reflection – The Visitors

Reading – 1 John 1:1-3

Reading – 1 Peter 1:10-12

A candle is lit

Prayer – for unexpected guests; for people who struggle with difficult questions.

Carol – Silent night, holy night

Reflection – Mary's baby, God's son

The final candle is lit

Prayer – thanking God for Jesus Christ, our Saviour.

Final carol – See him lying on a bed of straw (Calypso carol)

Blessing

Appendix Two – "Wonder: the Alternative Carol Service" Outline

Reflection – Part 1 – The Reason to wonder
NB. Start in pitch black. One light comes on.

A Hallelujah Christmas
(a Christmassy version of the Leonard Cohen classic, rewritten by Cloverton)

Welcome

Opening worship
- O come all ye faithful
- O come, O come Emmanuel

Hallelujah Christmas – Verse 1 – "I've heard about this baby boy"

Bible reading – Isaiah 9:2-7 *(to backing of Nimrod)*

Reflection – Part 2 – In the beginning was … hope

Carol – O holy night (performance)

Hallelujah Christmas – Verse 2 – "A couple came to Bethlehem"

Bible reading – Luke 2:1-7

Reflection – Part 3 – Bigger than the Universe

Carol – You stepped down from heaven (Adore)

Hallelujah Christmas – Verse 3 – "The shepherds left their flocks by night"

Bible reading – Luke 2:8-20

Reflection – Part 4 – Born to save

Carol – Hark the herald (King of heaven)

Hallelujah Christmas – verse 4 – "A star shone bright up in the east"

Carol – Noel (performance)

Reflection – Part 5 – Come and see

A Hallelujah Christmas – Verse 5 – "I know You came to rescue me"

Final Carols (Congregation)
- Ding dong Merrily on high (The Celebration's Starting)
- Joy to the world (Unspeakable joy)

Blessing and Dismissal

Appendix Three – "At the Heart of Christmas: The Alternative Carol Service" Outline

This service used material from "Remembering with Mary as well as "One heart, one life, one love", which was written specifically for this service.

Heartbeat / Genesis 1 + John 1 (intro of "Noel" playing)

In the beginning
In the beginning God created the heavens and the earth.
The Word was with God, and the Word was God.
Now the earth was formless and empty, darkness was over the surface of the deep,
The Word was in the beginning with God.
and the Spirit of God was hovering over the waters.
God said, 'Let there be light'; and there was light.
All things came into being through him... What has come into being through him was life, and the life was the light of all people.
God saw that the light was good; and God separated the light from the darkness.
The light shines in the darkness...
God called the light Day, and the darkness he called Night.
The light shines in the darkness, and the darkness did not overcome it.

Carol: Noel (performance)

Welcome

Opening worship – 2 songs
- O come all ye faithful

- Hallelujah Christmas (Cloverton)

Reflection – One heart, one life, one love

Bible reading – The Heart

The heart is deceitful above all things and beyond cure. Who can understand it? 'I the Lord search the heart and examine the mind, to reward each person according to their conduct, according to what their deeds deserve.'
(Jeremiah 17:9-10)

I will give them a heart to know me, that I am the Lord. They will be my people, and I will be their God, for they will return to me with all their heart. (Jeremiah 24:7)
You will seek me and find me when you seek me with all your heart.
(Jeremiah 29:13)

'This is the covenant that I will make with the people of Israel after that time,' declares the Lord. 'I will put my law in their minds and write it on their hearts. I will be their God, and they will be my people.
(Jeremiah 31:33)

I will give them an undivided heart and put a new spirit in them; I will remove from their heart of stone and give them a heart of flesh.
(Ezekiel 11:19)

Carol – O little town of Bethlehem (pre-record) (cong.)

Bible reading – Luke 1:26-38

Reflection – How it all began

Bible Reading: Matthew 1:18-25

Bible reading – Luke 2:1-7

Reflection – Arriving in Bethlehem

Carol In the bleak midwinter (performance)

Bible Reading – Luke 2:8-20

Reflection – The Visitors

Carol – Make room (cong.)

Bible Reading – John 1:9-14

Reflection – Mary's baby, God's son

Conclusion

In amidst the whirlwind of the shepherds and angels, in the midst of the chaos of the birth – in all of this, Mary took time to ponder. She treasured up all these things in her heart. I want to invite us all to do that today. In the midst of the chaos we face, when all around is unexpected, may we find the wonder of God with us – God come near to us. May we hear the heartbeat of the one who loved us so much he became human for us. May we still our hearts and allow ourselves to hear his heart beating for us – and may his heart beat in and through us. And may we receive his love into our hearts. Before we sing our final carols, let's take a few moments of silence.

Final Carols (Congregation)
- Joy to the world (Unspeakable joy)
- Ding dong

Blessing and Dismissal